MW01259099

Best wishes Hope you enjoy Dylan Stafford

Daddy Muscles

A First-Time Father's Diary
Of Marriage, Pregnancy, Parenthood
And
A Second Chance to Become a Real Man

By Dylan Stafford

Daddy Muscles: A First-Time Father's Diary of Marriage, Pregnancy, Parenthood and a Second Chance to Become a Real Man / by Dylan Stafford. 1st ed.

ISBN 978-0-557-51547-9

In honor of my parents, Ginny and Jack Stafford,
married-happily-ever-after since June 7, 1965.

Thanks Mom and Dad.

And to Marisa and Jackson,
you are the loves of my life
and none of this would matter without you.

I love you.

Introduction

This book is a second chance for me. I had a dream of being a writer in my teens, but put it off for *someday*. Many years later, my wife Marisa and I were trying to start our family. We had a brief pregnancy and then had trouble getting pregnant a second time. Grateful when the spark lit, I started jotting down observations of what was happening, writing short stories and sharing them with family and friends.

Maybe that's as far as it would have gone, a shoebox full of essays to give to our son when he turned 18, or to his future fiancée someday. But in 2009, things changed. My wife left her job of 20 years. Then California ran out of money again and my state salary shrank. In four short months, our household income dropped by half, just like so many families right now. The pressure pushed me and I dusted off the dream of being a writer. With some heavy lifting, that shoebox became *Daddy Muscles*.

My team for this effort has been fantastic. Natalie (Bich Ngoc Thi) Le helped me get started by connecting me to Nancy Marriott who provided me coaching and editing and nurturance. Julian Ryder and Andy Frank and their team gave the book its look and feel. Thanks Andy, for finding a stunt-double for the bicep on the cover. Neal Abramson and I supported each other as we both wrote our books. Thanks Paul Turro, for telling me to go to the ranch and write; it took a while, but here it is. Thanks Everett, for teaching me about gratitude and appreciating what is on my plate. Many friends and family have nudged me forward, none more than my wife Marisa.

It's been a transformative journey, reflecting on the people who've made my life what it is. *It takes a village to raise a child*, the saying goes. It takes a village to raise a man too.

Life now, being married and being a father, is the best thing that's ever happened to me. *Daddy Muscles* is my attempt to share my gratitude for the village that raised me—for my parents and teachers. My intention is to make you laugh, to make you smile and to share some life with you. I think we all do best when we share and I'm sharing to say thanks. I wrote this book for my angel wife Marisa, for our little miracle son, Paul Jackson Bonaventure Stafford, and for my parents.

Thanks for the chance to be a husband and a daddy and a son.
I love you,

Dylan

Culver City, California, 2010

Table of Contents

ONCE UPON A TIME ~ MARISA

DADDY DIARIES ~ FORTY ONE WEEKS

DADDY DIARIES ~ YEAR ONE

ONCE UPON A TIME ~

MARISA

Wedding Providence

A full moon shone the night I married my bride Marisa. It was October 10, 2003, and we were in our mid-30s, both of us getting married for the first time.

Everyone at our wedding party flew in through the Providence airport to get to our Rhode Island wedding, bringing blessings for our big day. *Providence* is the foreseeing care of God over the creatures of the earth, and looking back, that's what it felt like for me to be getting married to Marisa and starting a new life with her.

Rhode Island wasn't a convenient location for a wedding, but it's where my bride wanted to get married. Marisa had moved to Los Angeles the year before, following her promotion to senior director in a large hotel company; I followed her shortly thereafter. Marisa had grown up in New Jersey where most of her family lived, while I grew up in Texas, where my family lived. To entice family and friends into coming to our Rhode Island wedding, we promised brilliant fall foliage. But on our wedding weekend, it was as green as July.

As soon as we'd found a location for both ceremony and reception, I called my folks about our plans.

"Son, I know it's your wedding, and we want you to be happy ... but have you thought about getting married somewhere closer?" my dad asked. "Like maybe somewhere here in Texas?"

My father is a native citizen of Texas, that proud country between the U.S. and Mexico. Semi-retired now, he prefers to travel in his Chevy Suburban, making weekend trips to his ranch with his multiple toolboxes and his Border collie *Dottie Girl* in the back. He always carries a Leatherman multi-tool on his belt and has the MacGyver-like ability to fix almost anything. He delivered my younger sister Lisa in the back seat of a Volkswagen Squareback when the car ran out of gas on the way to the hospital. For him, going through airport security, and therefore leaving behind his tools, his dog, and his Suburban is not much fun, even less so after 9/11.

My mom is a transplant to Texas. She spent her childhood in Illinois and later Arizona. She still sometimes calls herself a desert gal, but she left Arizona a long time ago on a slow train ride to attend Trinity University in San Antonio. She met my dad on a blind date, and she's lived in Texas ever since.

Mom and Dad live in Fort Worth now, but in the 1970s, they raised my brother, sister and me in a tired, Texas railroad town called Denison. Located on the Red River, that jagged border between Texas and Oklahoma, Denison was not known for much when I was a kid. Dwight Eisenhower was born there, his birthplace now a museum a few blocks away from where my childhood friend Steve grew up. We had the Denison Dam forming Lake Texoma, and Steve's dad was old enough to remember chain gangs of German prisoners helping to build the dam during World War II. In the movie *The Last Picture Show*, when Cybill Shepherd's character Jacy tries to elope, they are heading for Lake Texoma.

Denison got another famous son in January of 2009, when Chesley Sullenberger landed his plane in the Hudson River. He graduated from Denison High School in 1969, the year I was born and 18 years before I graduated from the same school. My best friend Travis was taught first grade by Sully's mom. That's Denison, a BB-gun-fishing-pole-hot-dogs-and-firecrackers kind of town, a real-life version of Anarene, the imaginary Texas town in *The Last Picture Show*.

I continued on talking to my dad, hoping to convince him that Rhode Island wasn't such a bad idea.

"Dad, it's Marisa's dream to have a wedding in the open, and her friend Patty got married at a place called the Glen Manor House, right on the banks of the Sakonnet River. I think you and mom would like it. It's wooded and peaceful and beautiful."

Silence on the other end. And then, a small concession: "I guess we can make it," my dad said haltingly. "But you know how much I hate to fly….."

****

Marisa was raised a "cradle Catholic," meaning she was born into the religion not converted, in the state of New Jersey. She went to the University of Rhode Island and while there fell in love with the smallest state in the union. Her college priest at URI, Father Randy, still served in the area and agreed to perform our wedding. We booked the Glen Manor House, just outside of Providence and close to Newport. We sent a save-the-date email to our friends and family.

All was going well until the Catholic Diocese of Providence announced that no, an outdoor wedding would not be an official Catholic wedding. The reception could be held anywhere, but the service itself had to be inside a church building.

Marisa was upset. She had dreamed of an outdoor wedding her whole life. "God is everywhere, right?" she said in exasperation. "God made the trees and the grass, too. How come we can't have an outdoor wedding?"

"Honey, they spent a lot of money on all those churches," Marisa's mother Barbara replied. "And they want to use them." Barbara raised five children, and she always looks at things pragmatically.

"Jeez. I can't believe we'd have this much hassle in New Jersey. We ought to write a letter," Marisa's father Paul suggested.

Paul is the big personality, an energetic Jersey guy who loves family, golf and celebrating. He was a physical education coach for his entire career, only to semi-retire to South Carolina and become a small business owner. When I met Marisa he was running two Dunkin' Donuts in Charleston.

During our courtship in 2002, whenever the topic of marriage came up, Marisa let me know I'd have to ask Paul's permission formally before proposing to her. I agreed but just how I would do this remained vague.

Then Marisa and I took a trip to Germany together, so I could show her Munich and the friends I'd made in the three years I'd worked there with a global technology company called Siemens. We were staying at my friend Oliver's apartment and I planned to take Marisa to a romantic medieval walled city that miraculously hadn't been bombed in World War II, called Rothenburg ob der Tauber.

It seemed as good a time as any. Using a calling card, I dialed internationally several times before reaching the Dunkin' Donuts in Mount Pleasant, South Carolina.

"Um, hello, yeah, could I speak with Paul please, the owner?" My heart was racing and I was nervous. I waited a while until finally he came on the phone.

"Dunkin' Donuts, this is Paul. How can I help you?" Marisa's dad had lived in the south for a few years by now, but his Jersey accent was alive and well.

"Hi Paul, um, Mr. Szem. This is Dylan calling from Germany. Everything is okay and Marisa and I are having a great trip. I'm sorry to bother you at work, but I wanted to ask you a question."

"Sure, Dylan. What's up?"

Sitting cross-legged on the cold tile floor in the bathroom of Oliver's apartment, I took a breath and mustered my courage. The phone cord snaked under the door which I'd closed to get some privacy. It was almost 1:00 a.m. in Munich, and Marisa was asleep in the other room.

"Well, um," I moved my lips but no words were coming out. Finally, I blurted, "Yes, well. Marisa and I have been dating for over a year now, as you know, and we get along really well and we really like each other and we want to get married and... I'm calling you to ask you for your blessing. I want to ask Marisa to marry me."

There was a moment of silence on the line, and for a second I thought the call had dropped. Then came the voice of my future father-in-law.

"Well, this is great news. Welcome to the family. Her mother and I are happy to say *Yes*."

My relief must have been palpable, even some 4,000 miles away. We talked for a few minutes more. After I hung up, I was so high, I came in and nudged Marisa awake.

"I did it. I asked him!" I said trying to control my volume. "He said yes! Your dad said yes!"

"Of course he said yes, love," Marisa replied groggily. "And I'm proud of you. Good job. Now let's get some sleep."

But it took a while for me to calm down and fall asleep that night. Now that the door was open, I had some thinking to do.

The next day we drove a rental car from Munich to Rothenburg and spent the day wandering the quiet, quaint streets that hadn't changed since before Columbus sailed the ocean blue. A park stood on one edge of the city, high on a bluff with a wide, lookout view of the river below. Marisa and I stopped at a bench under an ancient Linden tree, protected by its canopy from a light afternoon drizzle.

I looked around and realized the park was empty, a surprising occurrence for such a popular tourist destination. I took the moment as a sign, and sliding off the bench and onto one knee, took her hand and looked deeply into her eyes.

We smiled at each other and I began. "Marisa, my love, will you marry me? Will you allow me to be your husband?"

"Yes Dylan. I will marry you. I will be your wife."

We kissed and then sat together for some time, holding each other under the Linden tree in a timeless moment neither of us will ever forget.

****

My future in-laws, the Szems, shortened from *Szemplenski*, were a very different family than the one I'd grown up in. Marisa's great grandfather, Roman, came to America from Poland through Ellis Island, where she'd seen his name listed in the passenger archives. Today, the Szems are a big, boisterous, Catholic, New Jersey family. My Texas, Protestant family is smaller in size and decibels.

The first time I met Marisa's family en masse was 10 months into our dating, at Easter in 2002. I flew into New Jersey for the weekend where the whole family convened for a big Easter Sunday celebration. We went to church while a roast cooked in the oven, and we came home to the smells of a feast. All eight cousins, aged six to sixteen, were there and ran wild through the house with some neighbor kids mixed into the pack.

It was a challenge, meeting everyone for the first time. Marisa's oldest brother, Chris, is a tall, tan, successful guy with blue eyes and a mega smile. Chris and his wife Lisa have five children. You'd never miss Lisa when she enters a room, as she dresses Jersey bling and still proudly carries the bombshell figure of her youth. She sat me down on the couch, her glass of Pinot Grigio in hand, for a little get-to-know-ya conversation and looked me right in the eye.

"So, I hear you don't have a job. Is that right?" she asked.

It was a fair and accurate question, presented in direct, New Jersey fashion, but it took everything in me to not run screaming from the room. My whole Texas-nice, small-town, small-family background was getting blown up in the face of northeast, in-your-face, big family living and one simple question.

My desire to make a good impression was at odds with the fact that I'd been out of work almost six months, since getting laid off from Siemens after 9/11. Kids were running around and wine was flowing, and grandparents and great grandparents were milling around in the background, but at that moment it was just Lisa and me on the couch. I was alone with a chorus of voices in my head.

"Yes, that's right," I replied, getting my focus. "I got laid off after 9/11. My whole team got let go. I've been looking for something up here in New Jersey, with the hope of moving to be near Marisa. But now she's getting promoted to Los Angeles, so I'm about to start a whole new job search out there."

Lisa became a great sister-in-law. She's a dynamo mother to her five kids. I doubt she even knew her question felt like hazing to my indirect, southern self. She was just getting the low down on the new kid dating her husband's sister. It was a moment, and I didn't run away panicked but rather answered the question fairly and enjoyed the rest of the day.

After dinner, Marisa organized the entire multi-generation crew into a massive Easter Egg hunt while simultaneously photo-journaling the proceedings with her big safari camera equipped with a telephoto lens. She'd had 16 years of being the super-aunty, and I got to see my future wife's formidable people management skills on display that Easter Sunday.

But it would take more than Marisa's well-honed people skills to sway the Catholic Diocese of Providence some months later to allow us to have our wedding outdoors on the lawn of the Glen Manor House. With my future father-in-law at the helm, and help from Marisa's whole family, we crafted a letter requesting an exception and submitted it to the Diocese of Providence. We pleaded our case that an outdoor wedding was Marisa's dream and also that of our out-of-state, elderly guests would have difficulty navigating unfamiliar back roads, going between different locations for wedding and reception.

The letter worked, but with a wrinkle. We had mentioned in passing that I had grown up a preacher's kid, the son of an ordained Presbyterian minister. The answer we got back was that we could be granted a "dispensation from canonical form"–basically an exception to the rule—as long as my dad would receive the vows. Father Randy's presence would make the ceremony officially Catholic, if my dad co-officiated and received the vows.

We were overjoyed. We could be outside! It could all happen! And now my own childhood dream had a chance of coming true, as well. As a preacher's kid, I'd always assumed my father would perform my wedding. It all sounded good.

The only remaining problem was that my dad didn't want to do it. I had already asked him to marry us a few months earlier, before this latest hook made his participation a requirement, and he'd declined. I'd asked him at Thanksgiving dinner with my mom, my fiancée and my sister Lisa watching. Presumptuously, I had already promised Marisa that Dad would say yes. It hadn't crossed my mind that there was anything else to do but ask.

"Son, your wedding is your day, and I don't want to be the center of attention. I'm semi-retired and my eyesight isn't that good anymore. Besides, I don't know the setting, and if it's okay with you, I would really rather not."

I had nodded and stared at my plate. I had on my best game face, but I could feel my cheeks turn red. I was embarrassed, because I had assured Marisa that my dad would agree to marry us, and I was angry because he had now said no.

Why couldn't he just say yes? And it wasn't "okay" with me—not at all. I very much wanted Dad to perform my wedding ceremony and in that moment at the dinner table, he declined my request. With my face feeling hotter by the second, I did my best to honor my dad and my fiancée, and not say anything to turn my disappointment into something worse. I had so expected him to say yes that I actually had nothing else to say. I just sat there, looking at my food.

This reaction I had surprised me. In typical Texas-guy fashion, I hadn't thought much about my wedding day. I'd probably spent much more time fantasizing about a wedding night, but for the day, I assumed the woman I married would have a bunch of ideas and plans and everything would go best if I just went along with as many of them as possible. I figured I would probably wear a tuxedo and that my dad would be standing up at the front of the church asking us to say "I do." As a preacher's kid, I grew up watching my dad in church. If the doors were open, we were there. He gave sermons. He officiated at funerals. He ran church camps and directed the choir. People listened to him, and he was my hero. He performed the weddings of my cousins, and I always assumed he would do my wedding, too.

Now he had said no, that he would rather not.

It's hard when you're a kid and your parent disappoints you. It's even harder when you are an adult and you are disappointed, because then you feel like a kid again. The only other time I remember wanting something this badly—and this is maybe not a fair comparison—was in 8th grade. My best friend Travis invited me to see a Van Halen concert in Dallas. Travis' dad was going to get concert tickets and drive us. All I had to do was get permission from my dad to join them. I've known Travis since we were three. As kids we used to play at being the Lone Ranger and Kemosabe, and even today we still leave each other voicemails, *Hey Kemosabe, give me a call…*

Dad and I had been working together for a couple months converting the attic into a bedroom for me. It was a big project with lots of custom fitting of wood panels and holding of flashlights. Before I asked permission to go to the Van Halen concert, which seemed like forever, I was the super-helper. I was terrified my dad might say no, and I'd have to stay home while my best friend went to a real rock concert and came home with a real concert t-shirt, the most amazing trophy my 8th grade brain could imagine. My plan to improve my odds was to butter up my dad by being the best father's helper in the world, before I mustered the courage to ask.

I finally did ask, and Dad said yes. The 1982 Van Halen Diver Down tour was my first rock concert and a highlight of my teen years. David Lee Roth was his lion-mane, high-kicking best. Eddie Van Halen was the guitar god of the day. It was a pilgrimage to rock and roll and the possibility of being cool. I kept that concert t-shirt all the way to college before I finally lost it. I'd probably still wear it now, or have it mounted on a wall under a spotlight, if it hadn't disappeared.

But this time Dad said no, and here I was, all grown up and about to get married, feeling like the Thanksgiving turkey. I was mad at my dad, stuffing my emotions out of fear of making a disappointment even worse. And this time, there was no way to butter Dad up and make him change his answer. He and I lived in different states and we weren't working on any attic conversions. I had asked and he'd declined. My dad is a straight-shooter, and I knew he told me exactly what he thought—*our day, the spotlight, his eyesight.* I also knew that at some cosmic level, it would work out if he didn't officiate at my wedding. We'd still get married without him. But I was mad and disappointed and embarrassed, anyway.

Now, the game had changed, and four months after that Thanksgiving visit, we had a new wrinkle in our plans to deal with from the Diocese of Providence. The letter said that the only way we could get married outside of a church was for my dad to co-officiate at the ceremony.

We hadn't asked for that. We'd only asked for approval for Father Randy to conduct our wedding outside.

This meant I'd have to ask Dad again.

I called him from California. "Hey Dad, how is it going?"

"We're all fine here, but it's dry. We wish it would rain down at the ranch, but up here in Fort Worth we're doing fine." It was the usual Texas weather update.

"Dad, remember how I was telling you about that letter we sent to the Catholic Church, asking permission to have an outdoor wedding?"

"Yeah, how is that going? Have you heard back?"

"Well, yeah, actually, we did get a letter back. We'd asked for permission for Father Randy to officiate outside." I paused a moment. "But they wrote that it could only happen outside if you would join him and co-officiate." There, I'd said it.

Silence.

I continued, "We didn't ask for that, but we mentioned in passing that you were a minister. They said you would need to receive the vows, since we won't be in a Catholic church. Father Randy can be there to add the Catholic part, but it's kind of like we need you to make the whole thing work." I paused again, but he was still listening, so I kept going.

"I know you said that you would rather not because of your eyes and the travel and this being our day and you not wanting to be the focus of attention, but this would really mean a lot to us if you could do it. It's Marisa's childhood dream to have an outdoor service." There, I'd said that part, too, and for better or for worse, I had now asked a second time. I didn't tell him it was also my dream to have him officiate at my wedding, even though it was.

The pause seemed long in my mind.

"Well, son, I would love to help out." He was saying the words, but I couldn't believe I was hearing them. He continued, "If my officiating can help make the day a success, then I would be honored to help. Tell me about Father Randy, is he a nice guy? I'm sure he is…"

That was it. The wind had shifted back in our favor, first the dispensation and now my dad saying yes.

This was February. The rest of the year was taken up with the wedding details. We had agreed to split the expenses of the wedding with Marisa's dad. Paul would pick up half the tab, and Marisa and I would split the rest between us. My own money was tight, and I was trying to make a good impression on my fiancée, but I wasn't sure how I could keep up my part of the arrangement.

It wasn't that I didn't have income potential, exactly. In 1995, I'd received a Master of Business Administration (MBA) degree from the University of Chicago, one of the best business programs in the world. My post-MBA job was in human resource consulting with Siemens, a global German technology company. I had worked in Santa Clara, California for two years, and been promoted to the world headquarters in Munich, Germany for three years. In 2001, I was assigned to a global change management team, a position that involved a lot of travel and allowed me to live anywhere. Re-visiting my Texas roots, I'd gotten an apartment in Fort Worth near my parents.

In May of 2001, I signed up for a course on personal productivity that was offered on a cruise ship while touring the Mediterranean. It was on that cruise that I met Marisa, and back on land, we began to date long distance, me in Texas and her in New Jersey.

And then 9/11 happened. Six weeks after 9/11, I was laid off from Siemens, along with the entire team. I continued dating Marisa long distance, and almost a year later, in August of 2002, when she relocated to Los Angeles, I moved there to be with her.

Eventually, I found an entry-level job in the UCLA Anderson School of Management, making only about half of what Marisa was making. My situation was even more tenuous, because I'd used much of my savings in the nine months since my lay off. But none of this seemed to faze Marisa. Years later, while she was watching the TV show *Say Yes to the Dress*, I realized her wedding dress had never shown up on the wedding budget. Marisa had quietly paid for it on her own—a beautiful gown with Swarovski crystal beading on the bodice, the price of which I would only dare ask six years into our marriage.

Marisa and her dad both have a let's-make-it-work attitude about money. Having just gone nine months without a paycheck, I had a let's-stretch-it-out attitude about cash. It was during this pre-job period for me that Marisa and I visited Rhode Island to scout out wedding locations. The first place she took me to was a palatial estate that had been used for the final party scene in the movie *Meet Joe Black*.

I did a double take as we walked onto the expansive lawn. "Marisa, you *do* remember that I don't have a job right now?" I said, trying not to sound too cheap. "Do we really need enough acreage to land helicopters?"

"My grandma married my granddad when he didn't have a job. I'm not worried about you," she chimed, optimistic as ever.

Later I thought maybe she'd set me up on purpose, so that after the shock of the palatial movie set option, any other choice would seem modest by comparison, and I would automatically say yes. It was all fun to Marisa. Jersey people love shopping, and we were shopping for wedding locations. For me, even the smaller mansion we saw next, the Glen Manor House, seemed like a stretch. Not wanting to disappoint her, I signed on, and our search was over.

While Marisa planned the wedding, I wondered about a bachelor's party. I wanted to have one, but there were two problems. The first was that my friends were scattered all over the world. The second was that I had been in recovery for two years, having quit drinking two months before I met Marisa. Things had gotten pretty bad before my mom and sister Lisa rallied the family and did an intervention on me, and it had worked. Now I knew I had to have a sober bachelor's party, but I didn't want to ask people to fly in from all over to watch me drink iced tea. When you get on a plane for a bachelor's party, you expect something spicier than tea.

I was trying to honor the principles of sobriety in all my affairs, which was part of the reason I had taken the entry level job at UCLA. I was afraid if got a "big shot" job, I might not be able to stay sober. Marisa had a big promotion bringing her to Los Angeles, and I felt that two big jobs under one roof might be more than I could handle. It was too important for me now, about to be married, to blow it and fall off the wagon.

I finally decided on a small bachelor's party with my dad, brother Jon, and cousin Charlie at Dad's ranch in the middle of central Texas. Some of my favorite childhood memories had happened at the ranch. We'd spend time with his parents, Bobby and Harold Dear, as well as his brother Bill's family, sitting around a campfire or going fishing and hunting. Later in life, after Dad inherited his part of the ranch, it became an even more important retreat for him, and we spent many more Thanksgiving family holidays there.

I wanted my bachelor's party to be another memory at the ranch I could look back on, and as things turned out, it was. We bought a 12-foot tall Bur Oak from a nursery and planted it in the front of the ranch house, christening it the *Wedding Tree*. We ate steaks and told stories, my perfect bachelor's party. I had bought a pack of Marlboro Lights—I don't smoke, but I used to bum cigarettes when I drank—and after everyone had gone to bed, I walked out into a pasture under the big, black Texas sky and smoked a cigarette. My head felt the rush as the nicotine hit my brain, the effect amplified since I so rarely smoke.

My sober life was much slower than life in my drinking days, and this simple moment was as much excitement as my bachelor's party required. I rubbed out the ember, put the butt in my pocket and listened to the night sounds. I said a prayer of gratitude that I'd learned in sobriety for the chance to get married, looking at the far away stars and pondering how my life was turning out, living in Los Angeles and marrying a Jersey gal.

****

The wedding weekend arrived, and dedicated family and friends made the long journey to Rhode Island to gather on the bank of the Sakonnet River. Oliver, Lutz, Bärbel and other friends I'd made living and working in Germany flew in from Europe, not quite arriving in the middle of the brilliant New England fall foliage we'd hoped for. Many of my college buddies from Texas A&M University couldn't attend, because they were serving in the Iraq war.

We got married on the lawn of the Glen Manor House, the river flowing quietly alongside our gathering, at 4:00 in the afternoon. It rained lightly an hour before the ceremony but cleared in time to wipe off the chairs. Twenty minutes before the ceremony, I was standing in a hallway of the main building with butterflies in my stomach. I asked my dad to stand guard while I went into a side room to have a quiet moment. I knelt and said the Lord's Prayer. I asked God to go into the marriage before me, to take the lead and show me the way. It was another prayer I had learned in recovery about asking for help. I calmed down. I stood up. I came outside and followed my father to the front of the field to wait for my bride.

My sister Lisa was a bridesmaid and my mom was seated in the front row, beaming. Travis and Roger, my other oldest friend, were there. We've all known each other since we were three years old in preschool at St. Luke's Episcopal Church in Denison. Travis was my best man, and Roger sang the *Ave Maria*. Marisa's mom cried as Roger's baritone voice carried across the lawn. My other groomsmen were my brother Jon, my cousin Charlie, and Humberto, my roommate from college in our senior year. We men stood at the front as Roger finished singing, my Dad standing in the center. Father Randy had woken with a debilitating fever and my dad shouldered the whole load.

I could see Marisa's silhouette framed between the tall columns in the back. The warm chords of Pachelbel's Canon in D began to play. Marisa emerged from the shadows escorted by her father who stood tall and proud with his youngest daughter. In the soft, after-the-rain sunlight, Marisa looked like she was floating down the aisle, so gently was she taking her steps.

Arriving at the front, Paul lifted her veil and gave her a kiss. Marisa's shoulders were bare and she wore long white gloves up to the elbow. She handed her bouquet to Patty, her maid of honor, and our hands came together, gently squeezing hello. Her blue-green eyes sparkled and danced, and I could feel my own eyes tear up as the fullness of the moment washed over me, our moment that had finally arrived. Dad's words and prayers carried across the lawn in the late afternoon sunshine. Marisa and I exchanged our vows, and Dad received them. Our marriage had begun.

The reception was a blur with a few memorable moments. During Marisa's hotel career, she'd seen countless newlyweds miss the meal after being swept up in all the greeting and well-wishing. Not wanting that to be our fate, she arranged things so that we had a 20 minute pause to sit and savor each other and the dinner that our guests were enjoying.

Marisa danced with her dad, and I danced with my mom. Dancing without drinking is different for me, and I danced the entire evening, appreciating being sober and present to all of it. Marisa's Uncle Bob, a man at least 25 years older than me, danced towards me like he was trying out for the Olympics, doing some kind of Russian-looking, deep knee squats. He was grinning at me to join him, so I did a couple squats to be polite. A few minutes later, I realized I'd ripped a six inch hole in the seat of my tuxedo trousers. I was mortified until I realized the rip wouldn't show as long as I didn't do any high kicks the rest of the night.

We had splurged and gotten a band in honor of Marisa's grandfather, her dad's dad, a gifted, life-long piano player. The first time I met Alphonse and his wife Helen, he played piano after a family dinner, the talent in his fingers well-matched with his banter between songs. He was charismatic with his jokes and one-liners, and created a party every time he took the bench. Until the end of his life, he entertained several times a week for "old folks," ultimately playing for retirees much younger than he.

"Let me tell you the secret of a great marriage," Alphonse would start, pausing and looking around to make sure he had everyone's full attention. He acted as if he were bringing down the Word. "Every week, no matter what, we go out to a romantic dinner. Soft lights. Delicious food. Beautiful music." He paused, and then said, "Tuesday night, she goes. Thursday night, I go." *Baa daa bop.* He would smile and Helen would roll her eyes. They loved each other completely.

Alphonse lived to be 94. He and Helen were married 69 *glorious* years. At our wedding, she was 90 and he 91. Alphonse danced a dance with Marisa and I danced a dance with Helen. Two weeks after our wedding, Grandma Helen passed away, quickly and peacefully, with little warning.

After Helen passed, I remembered back to a tiny thought that had flashed in my mind during my wedding day dance with her. I thought she looked almost translucent, like the light was somehow going through her body at the edges. It was a silly thought, and in all the commotion of the wedding, it passed as quickly as it came. But then two short weeks later, as we paid our last respects, I remembered that vision and wondered if she, a very prayerful woman, had asked God for just enough time on earth to share our wedding day before moving on. I wondered if maybe God hadn't granted her request and then given us a shimmering future-angel to bless our first day of marriage.

Marisa had arranged a chocolate fountain, and my only regret was I danced so much I missed getting even a tiny taste of it. Marisa's college librarian Sue made our wedding cake, and Ray, her husband, filmed the day. Towards the end of the evening, my brother Jon found Marisa and me and took us out onto the huge expanse of lawn to see the full moon rising over the river. A shimmering ribbon of light played on the moving water, lighting the way for our future, it seemed. It was the perfect ending to the perfect wedding, ripped pants and all.

Providence is the foreseeing care of God over the creatures of the earth, and it is a righteous word to characterize all that had led up to that first day of our union. God allowed this "aw-shucks" Texas boy to fall in love with this cruise-missile-direct Jersey gal. She likes mayonnaise, while I grew up on Miracle Whip. She uses real butter, me margarine. If we'd never taken that personal productivity course on the cruise ship in the Mediterranean, we'd have never met each other and this day would never have happened. But God let us find each other and start our life together, and I felt blessed indeed to have a future so full of new possibilities.

The First Time (Century Tree)

In the fall of 2004, a year into our marriage, Marisa and I went to Texas for Thanksgiving with my family. Marisa had never been to my Alma Mater, so we drove the three hours from Fort Worth down to Aggieland, as Texas A&M is affectionately known, to visit. It was Wednesday of Thanksgiving week, and the campus was quiet. We wandered and I reminisced. I showed her the quad, the home of the Corps of Cadets, where I'd spent all four of my years as a "CT." Officially, CT stood for Cadets in Training, but internally we called ourselves Corps Turds. I explained to Marisa that at A&M it was actually quite an honor to be a CT; how we commissioned 13,000 officers for World War II, more than any other school including the U.S. Military Academy; how I wore a uniform all four years. We saw the Memorial Student Center. We went to the *Dixie Chicken*, the famous watering hole on the north side of the campus with its sticky floors, domino tables, and live rattlesnakes lounging in a big aquarium.

Texas A&M University was the first public institution of higher education in the great state of Texas. It was originally called the Agricultural and Mechanical College of Texas, but along the way it became Texas A&M University. We call the school "A&M," and we call ourselves "Aggies." I chose A&M because my Denison friend since fifth grade, Steve, was going there, and because I got a scholarship. Steve and I were both National Merit Scholars, which triggered an amazing amount of college material in the mail. After our junior year in high school, we attended the U.S. Naval Academy summer invitational. The year was 1986 and *Top Gun* fever infected every plebe and every upperclassman to dream of landing planes aboard aircraft carriers to fight the Russians. I loved the camaraderie of the Naval Academy cadets, but when recruiters explained the commitment, I balked. They told us we would serve in the Navy until the age of 27, which was ten years more than my 17 year old brain could imagine. What if something came along better before I was 27? I didn't pursue admission.

Instead I chose Texas A&M and horrified my grandmother. My dad's mom was named Bartlette but my oldest cousin couldn't pronounce her name and so instead she became "Bobby Dear." Bobby Dear was the youngest of three daughters, her father a doctor in the small town of Groesbeck, Texas. She was a redhead and met my grandfather when they were both students at Baylor University in the late 20s and early 30s.

Unbeknownst to me, in 1926 there had been an altercation at a football game between Texas A&M and Baylor. At halftime a riot had broken out and one Aggie student was hit by a chair and later died from his injury. Members of the Corps were so upset that they returned to College Station, mounted a cannon on a train, stole an engine and were off to attack the Baylor campus. The legend is that the Texas Rangers intervened and stopped the train. The two teams had a four year moratorium on all athletic competitions, but the bitter feelings lasted much longer, all the way to 1987 when Bobby Dear learned that I was going to Texas A&M and that I was joining the Corps of Cadets. On my next visit to her home in Dallas she took me aside for a very serious talk.

"Now Dylan, I want you to promise me, if ever you get into a bad situation at school, I want you to call me and say, 'Hi Grandma, how are the quail at the ranch?' That will be our secret code. If you call me and ask about the quail at the ranch, I will call your daddy and he will be able to go and help you."

I had no idea what she was talking about. I knew I was joining something big in the Corps of Cadets, and I had some suspicions that there could be hazing-type things happening, but I didn't know anything about the 1926 riot so I didn't understand Bobby Dear's fear. From her point of view as a Baptist Baylor Bear, I was selling my soul to the heathens. And besides, the logistics made zero sense to me. Assuming I were being hazed, and assuming I could step away from the hazing for a moment to make a phone call, and assuming the "quail code" worked, my dad would still have to get in a car and drive five hours south to come to my rescue.

"Okay grandma. I promise. If I get into any trouble, I will call you and ask about the quail at the ranch." I said. If it made her feel better, I could play along with it.

The Texas A&M Corps of Cadets is the largest ROTC outside of the big military academies. The Corps offers the full cadet experience and all the bonding, but does not require pursuing a military career. We wore our uniforms seven days a week. It is a down-home, middle-class version of West Point or Annapolis. The A&M Corps doesn't have the same ratio of military officers to cadets as the academies do, and so it is less supervised and more wild-west in style. The Corps for me was an in-your-face experience, a lot of yelling, a lot of pushups, and a lot of fun in a *Full Metal Jacket* meets *Animal House* kind of way.

Most of us cadets were burger-fed Texas boys. In 1987, the Corps was primarily male and primarily white. There were 24 freshmen in my outfit, 22 white guys, one black guy and one Mexican, Humberto. Nowadays, as I walk the rainbow UCLA campus I'm amazed at the contrast to my youth.

We came from all over Texas, from the big cities of Houston, Dallas, Austin, El Paso and San Antonio, from the big suburbs of Plano and the Woodlands, and from the smaller towns of Sugarland and Pearland, Joshua and Denison. John Harlan came from the smallest town, the west Texas dot-on-the-map called Bula. When asked by the upperclassmen, "Where the hell is Bula?"

23

John replied, "Sir, Bula is near Muleshoe, Sir." Only James Thome was from out of state, and only Humberto was from out of the country.

The upperclassmen told us the first week in the Corps that our fellow classmates were to be called our *buddies*. I thought it was a joke when I first heard the word.

"*Buddy?* Isn't that from the 1950s? Wouldn't *Leave it to Beaver* have a *buddy?* No one seriously uses that word anymore, do they?"

"Why yes they do, *fish* Stafford, and so will you from now on. Your buddies are your responsibility, and you are their responsibility, and you better start acting that way."

Another word we were taught was *fish*. Freshmen at Texas A&M are always referred to as *fish*. I guess the etymology is *fish out of water*. The upperclassmen told us, "Your buddies will be the best men at your wedding. They will be the pallbearers at your funeral." We had to take them at their word, that August of 1987, hearing the induction as we sat in a hot hallway with our newly shaved, almost bald, fish haircuts. Humberto was the only cadet from Mexico, and he became one of my best friends. He proved the upperclassmen right when he came to Rhode Island to be a groomsman for me at my wedding.

The Corps gave me the camaraderie of the Naval Academy without the ten year military commitment. A&M was also an hour south of the ranch, and I could see myself spending weekends with my mom and dad there.

After I graduated from A&M, I worked one year as a recruiter for their Honors Program. There are no mountains or ocean near A&M, and I would joke with prospective students that the only natural attractions we had were heat, humidity, and the occasional tornado. That wasn't exactly true. We had sunsets, great college football and beautiful trees.

When A&M opened in 1876, it was situated on an open prairie with almost no trees. Today the huge, 5000 acre campus stretches westward and is covered with trees. The most magnificent of these are southern live oaks that line the main entrance to the campus and canopy the winding sidewalks. In the historic center of campus, in front of the Academic Building, there is one tree that has a special spot in the hearts of all Aggies, the Century Tree.

The Century Tree sprawls in all directions, having thrived for more than 100 years of growth on the A&M campus. The massive branches reach up and out, some extending all the way to the ground. It's a romantic and magical spot, like a tree you'd see in a *Harry Potter* movie. At the base of the trunk, there's a bench where many marriage proposals have been made. Nowadays you can Google it and find videos of proposals on YouTube. We didn't have that in my day.

****

In giving her the tour, I had shown Marisa everything I could think to show her. She had listened to four years of my memories and the tall tales that went with them. We strolled back through the center of the campus, and I showed her the one place we hadn't been to yet, the Century Tree.

"This is where I would have proposed to you if we had met during college," I remarked.

"Oh, really. It's that special of a place?" she asked.

"For sure, this is the heart of the campus." I said. "See over there, that bronze statue is of Lawrence Sullivan Ross, the man who founded Texas A&M. We all call him 'Sully.' He went to Baylor, but we don't talk about that. He was governor of Texas and then he retired and became president of A&M. He even kept the state from closing A&M at one point. The legend goes they were going to close A&M and convert it into an insane asylum—many contend they succeeded—when Sully punched out a legislator on the floor of the Texas Senate, yelling, "Don't you dare lay a hand on that little school on the Brazos

River." When I was a freshman in the Corps, we would run over before the sun came up with liquid Brasso and rags and polish Sully's statue."

It is never a good idea to ask an Aggie about A&M history, unless you have some time on your hands. I continued in full Aggie pride mode, "And here in the front of the Academic Building is where we hold Silver Taps, one of our most respected traditions."

"What is Silver Taps?" Marisa asked.

"Well, there are over 40,000 students studying here at any given time. As weird as it may seem, sometimes students die. They're young and all, but it's the law of averages with that many people. When a student passes away we have a special memorial right here in the middle of campus. We post a card with the person's name, class and major at the base of the flagpole. That night, students gather silently in the dark to pay their respect. At 10:30, there is a 21 gun salute by the Ross Volunteers, our honor guard. I was one of those honor guards. Then there is a bugle corps that plays a special version of taps known as Silver Taps. They play it three times, once each to the North, South and West. They don't play it to the East, because the sun will not rise on that Aggie again. Afterwards, everyone walks back to their dorms in silence. The whole ceremony takes place in the dark."

"Wow. What kind of school is this?" Marisa asked. "We didn't do things like that at the University of Rhode Island."

"Well, it's Aggieland. We're kind of big on traditions around here. If we do anything more than once, chances are we'll make it a tradition. Bigger even than Silver Taps is Aggie Muster. Every year on April 21st, the anniversary of the Battle of San Jacinto, we gather all over the world to remember Aggies who've passed away that year."

"Show me this bench, the one under the Century Tree." Marisa said.

We followed the sidewalk from Sully's statue over towards the oak and walked underneath its giant canopy. There was no one around the Wednesday night before Thanksgiving and we were alone at its base, the huge trunk anchored and holding its many branches. We sat down on the bench. "So this is where you would have proposed? This is that special place?" Marisa asked, a note of expectation in her voice.

"Uh huh," I replied. "I would have gotten on one knee and proposed right here. I would have been in my best Corps uniform, brass polished, boots shined, sharp haircut."

"Ooh, my Dilly in a uniform! I think I would have liked that." Marisa said and smiled. "So this is a good place for good news."

"The best."

"Well, I have some good news, Dylan." Marisa said, taking my hand and placing it lightly on her belly. "We're going to have a baby, you and me. I'm pregnant."

It was a shock. I had been lost remembering my college years and enjoying the romance of sharing all those memories. Now my bride was telling me something so special about our future. I cried a little, I was so moved in the moment. Then we laughed and hugged, and we kept our secret over the Thanksgiving weekend. We didn't tell my parents yet, as Marisa was barely a month along. She had missed her period, gotten tested, and found out she was pregnant.

"I have been waiting for a couple of days, trying to find the right, special moment to tell you," she said.

"Well you did a great job, my love. I will remember this moment for the rest of my life." I replied, touched by her sweetness.

****

We drove to the ranch the next day and had a Texas Thanksgiving weekend. Our turkey and trimmings came from Luby's Cafeteria, and we ate too much pumpkin pie. My brother Jon and I showed Marisa our childhood game called *hide the pie*. The idea is simple. First you serve yourself a piece of pie. Then you get as big a dollop of Cool Whip as possible with one over-sized spoon and plop it straight down. Whoever hides the pie most completely with just one dollop is the winner, hence the name *hide the pie*.

The ranch came to Dad through his grandfather, a country doctor in Groesbeck, Texas. His youngest daughter was his only redhead and his tomboy, my Baylor grandma Bartlette. My dad tells me Bobby Dear used to accompany her dad out into the country where he would graft pecan trees.

"She said he always wore gloves, to protect his delicate doctor's hands," Dad remembers. Bobby Dear passed away in the late summer of 1991, and my dad had a heart attack five days later. He recovered after heart surgery to find he'd inherited his mother's farm. Back in her day, cotton was grown on the farm, but these days cattle raising is better business.

Marisa and I took walks and talked, and I showed her my trees. Since college I have been planting trees on the ranch. I have planted over 400 trees but only have about 20 survivors to show for my work. I showed her the *Aggie Acre*, an area east of the ranch house that I fenced off and irrigated in 1993. I showed her the *Lutz Tree*, which we planted Thanksgiving of 1995 when my German friend Lutz visited. "This is what the politicians do when they visit Israel," I remember Lutz commenting as we broke the earth.

The ground is tough and the summers are hot. We have droughts and grasshoppers, and cattle eat the trees when they are small, but I do have some survivors. In my mind, planting trees is building for the future. It is a way to honor my family and do something to help my dad, even when I'm away living in Chicago or Palo Alto or Germany or Los Angeles. I have visions of my dad sitting in the shade of one of the trees I've planted.

This ain't Dallas…and this ain't Dynasty… went the old Hank Williams Jr. country song. Marisa had been properly forewarned that the ranch was rustic. The old ranch house is a shotgun shack built 70 years ago by sturdy people with meager resources. By 1992, it had fallen into disrepair when cattle had started to lean against it in the winters and puddle the water and soften the foundation. Dad and I spent a lot of weekends fencing it off, shoring up the foundation and re-roofing. The house kicks off water now, and you can warm it up in the winter, but it's far from the Taj Majal. *It still ain't Dallas….*but we love it. It's our family spot. It is a place to see the stars and hear the coyotes and build a campfire. We call it Spunky Flats, after the description in a local cemetery that describes how settlers referred to the area. The ground is claylike when it's wet, and turns to rock when it's dry.

My biggest surviving tree is a Choctaw pecan. The year I recruited for A&M, I drove to the ranch almost every weekend to work on the house with Dad. One weekend I brought Humberto with me, and we planted six pecans. Five of them died, but the Choctaw lived. Humberto and I planted them on a rainy day in May. He helped me finish the job, but only with a non-stop litany of complaints about gringos abusing Mexicans. That is how we talked to each other in the Corps, forever ragging on each other for grievances real or invented. Over two decades later, the pecan is casting real shade on the driveway, and it now has company from the Bur Oak *Wedding Tree.*

Humberto came to the U.S. at 18 and joined the Corps. His Corps nickname was *Paddington* because he was hairy all over and brown like a bear. I can't imagine doing the Corps in a second language or as a Mexican in the middle of white bread Texas, yet that is what Humberto did. I can't imagine being the shortest guy out of 2,200 cadets, but Humberto did that, too.

After turkey dinner and *hide the pie*, we watched college football on the 3-channel TV set in the ranch house. My Aggies lost the rivalry game with the t.u. (our nickname for the University of Texas) 26-13 in 2004. When I was in school, we beat t.u. often, but now it is rare. My freshman year of 1987 we beat them 20-13, won the Southwest Conference and beat Notre Dame and their Heisman Trophy-winning Tim Brown in the Cotton Bowl 35-10. In 1987, we were reportedly the largest incoming freshman class in the nation. It was said we ran out of teachers for freshman English, but we felt like kings.

Now, spending the whole weekend at the ranch with Marisa, I was dying to tell my mom and dad the pregnancy news but at the same time, I was savoring the secret. Marisa and I had not been trying to get pregnant. We were enjoying our first year together and trying to savor each other. If pregnancy happened it happened, but we were not in a hurry.

This felt right, finding out she that was pregnant in Texas, in the heart of Aggieland. Even Thanksgiving weekend added to the specialness. At Spunky Flats, Thanksgiving is one of the best weekends. I am forever nostalgic, and I love to look for connections between people and events, affirming they were meant to be. Marisa telling me under the Century Tree was perfect, my past connecting to our future.

****

Saturday night after Thanksgiving, we stayed at a hotel closer to Dallas/Fort Worth Airport to get our early flight out the next morning. Marisa wasn't feeling too well, so she stayed in the room that night while I went to have dinner with my other college roommate, Jeff, and his wife Pam. Jeff's now a successful civil engineer, but when we get together, it's like we are back in our college days. We lamented running out of time in the football game against t.u. Running out of time is another Aggie tradition. We have never lost a football game. We've run out of time, but we've never lost.

Jeff's dad Ronnie was in the Corps back in the late 1950s. Jeff's first nickname was *Yuckmouth*, for his freshman morning breath. Later, we changed it to *Old Army*, since he knew the most history about A&M, thanks to his dad.

While it is true that Jeff knew the most, I always had a suspicion that when he didn't know something, he wasn't afraid to guess, either.

We all loved Jeff's parents, Ronnie and Marge. Ronnie was an airline pilot for American Airlines, which meant his schedule had more flexibility than most of our parents. While most visiting parents would leave for home on Sunday afternoon, Ronnie and Marge often stayed an extra night on campus and left Monday morning. I watched them do this and told myself, "Someday that is the kind of dad I want to be. I want to have extra time."

Marge usually brought homemade cookies to start the weekend, and to finish it, Sunday night she and Ronnie would take a whole school of fish buddies out to dinner at Tom's Bar BQ, a greasy joint with dusty deer heads hanging from the walls and cold, long necked beer. The sliced brisket and sausage came out steaming hot, served not on a plate, but rather on butcher block paper, three layers thick. The only utensil you got was a wood-handled steak knife, heaven for your inner carnivore. The center of the table had a loaf of no-name white bread to share family style, plus Bar BQ sauce, pickles, and a big block of cheddar cheese to carve chunks from.

At Tom's, we ate with gusto, laughing, telling stories and relaxing, making fun of each other in the endless way we did, away from the quad and the upperclassmen and classes. Ronnie soaked it all in. Jeff and his older sister Sarah were both students at A&M, and being back on campus was one of the happiest places in the world for Ronnie. He never made us listen to his own tall tales of "old army days" even though we surely would have, grateful as we were to be treated to such a feast. I never thought about it then, but now I think he was hearing his own fish buddies from 30 years earlier echoed in us. I did realize that Ronnie was another model for how I wanted to live my life. I wanted to spend time with people I loved the way he did. His generous actions impressed on me the importance of slowing down to enjoy what you really love most.

When Jeff married Pam, he asked me to be his co-best man along with Brady. Brady turned out to be one of the coolest of all of the buddies, and we would elect him our outfit commander our senior year. Brady was one of those guys that other guys naturally listen to and respect. He wasn't flashy and he was unusually calm. One of four brothers, an athlete, and really smart in math, Brady became an F-15 pilot and flew in the first Gulf War, and he would fly again a decade later when we went back to Iraq. Our second foray into Iraq meant Brady had to miss my wedding to Marisa.

Jeff and Pam had adopted their two children from Russia, and they had all kinds of stories about the process. Jeff said the hardest part was actually seeing the orphanage in Russia, clean but grey and industrial. The children were in one big room with cribs in long rows, and when he saw them he wanted to take every one of them home with him. Jeff and Pam had to miss our wedding, not because of war, but because they had gotten *the call* and needed to make the transatlantic flights to adopt their second child, their son Jacob.

After visiting with Jeff and Pam, I headed back to the hotel room where Marisa had been resting. It was about 9:30 and I found Marisa awake and not looking well.

"Dylan, something's wrong," she said, looking scared. "I didn't want to call you during your dinner, but I don't feel well. I've had bleeding. Every time I go to the bathroom there's blood. There's lots of blood. We need to take me to a hospital."

I didn't know what to do. *Why hadn't she called me sooner?* I called the front desk and got the name of the best, closest hospital, and we went in a hurry. The hospital was in wealthy north Dallas, but we still sat for almost two hours waiting. Later, she told me it was the most frightened she'd ever been in her life, but I didn't know it then. They put us in an exam room where we sat for what seemed like an eternity. We weren't talking too much. It was hard to know which doctors and nurses were exactly doing what. They took blood and ran tests. The ultrasound was not finding anything. That was when it started looking bad. We waited. And we waited. And the news was not good.

The doctor was a young woman, roughly our age. "We won't be sure for a couple of days, but we think that this pregnancy may be ending. This happens sometimes. It is nature's way. You will be able to fly tomorrow and you will want to see your doctor, your OBGYN when you get back home."

"I don't even have an OBGYN yet," Marisa answered, sounding lost. "I just found out I was pregnant a few days ago. Isn't there something you can do?"

"The most important thing we can do is to make sure that you are okay. If the pregnancy is not going to sustain at this early stage, there is nothing we can do. Sometimes pregnancies don't sustain. There can be many different reasons. You didn't do anything wrong."

We took care of Marisa. We got back to the hotel room about 3:00 a.m. then home to California safely the next day. We hadn't been there long when Marisa called me into the bathroom. She wasn't crying, but almost.

"Look," she said pointing. "Do you think that's it?"

In the bottom of the toilet was a small, still pool of blood, and in the middle was a lump. In my mind I knew that in the first month of a pregnancy, there was only a cluster of cells, totally naked to the human eye. I told myself that I didn't know what we were seeing. I told myself that, but I couldn't help thinking there might be tiny little cells curled up in there somewhere, a little life that had ended.

"What do we do?" Marisa asked.

I honestly didn't know, but said, "We take care of you. That's what the doctor said to do."

Later I flushed the toilet. It felt harsh, like a scene from *Old Yeller*, like something people had to do in the frontier days when life and death came swift. I thought about my dad and how he always seemed so strong when there was a crisis. I tried to be strong. Together, Marisa and I said a prayer.

We found an OBGYN in Santa Monica and got Marisa scheduled for an exam. We got the results from Dallas and confirmed she was no longer pregnant. Marisa was going to be fine, but the pregnancy had not taken. We told our parents in the weeks that followed.

"Mom, Dad, are you on the speaker phone?" I asked.

"Yeah, son. How are things going?"

"Well, we have some news, but it is not good news. We didn't want to tell you yet. We got pregnant, but now we are not pregnant anymore." I wanted to say it quickly, not to get anything confused. I didn't want Mom to hear *pregnant* and get all happy, only to hear *not pregnant* in the next breath. I didn't want Mom to ride that particular roller coaster, and I didn't want Marisa to hear the ups and down of it either.

"Marisa got pregnant and we had just found out, but now the pregnancy has ended. Marisa is okay, and we have seen a doctor, but we wanted you to know."

"Oh, Marisa, we are so sorry. This has got to be hard for you," my parents said, offering us as much comfort as they could.

We told a few friends. We learned more people have had miscarriages than we ever imagined. It is nature's way we were told—repeatedly. The OBGYN we found told us of the five years of trying that he and his wife had been through.

"And see these guys right here?" he said, pointing to a photo of two children on his wall. "These guys are the fruits of those five years. Our kids. You guys hang in there. It will happen."

The time from Wednesday evening under the Century Tree to Saturday night in the hospital was not even a week, a short time from learning I was going to be a daddy to holding Marisa's hand in an emergency room. Marisa had only known about it a few days longer than me.

I thought a lot in those following weeks. I thought about the Century Tree, about Marisa putting my hand on her tummy, about hearing her say the words, *I'm pregnant.* I thought about how much I love A&M but how hard it was when I was there, being a freshman cadet away from home in a school with twice as many students as there were people in my hometown of Denison. I thought about Abraham Lincoln, creating future colleges for the country while we were tearing our country apart. I thought about droughts in Texas that could wither everything in sight, even full grown trees. I thought about acorns and how 99% of them never grow into trees.

Marisa and I had planted a seed. This particular seed had not taken root, but it had sparked, if even for a short while. We had been parents for a week.

Less Than a 2 Per Cent Chance

The doctor advised us to wait six months to let Marisa's body recuperate before we started trying to get pregnant again. We waited and then in 2005 we started. Marisa had to travel a lot with her work for a hotel company as senior director in charge of training and education. She loved the travel, but it made the baby-making game a challenge.

As we transitioned from recreation to procreation, sex got more scientific. We started to buy the ovulating kits to tell us the best time to get pregnant. Marisa got pregnant the first time without us even trying, so we thought with help from the kits getting pregnant a second time would be even easier. But that was not the case. Marisa's cycle was not consistent—18 days one month, 35 days the next. We went through over $500 of ovulating kits trying to find the right time between her work trips.

The months started to add up, but Marisa was still not getting pregnant. I got upset in the middle of 2005 when I learned that our health insurance was changing its policy in regards to fertility treatments. *Oh great, we're going to miss our chance to be parents because open enrollment only happens once a year,* I thought. *Or we'll have to go broke paying for in vitro on our own with no insurance support.* I knew from what Jeff had told me that *in vitro* wasn't cheap.

Marisa started seeing a fertility doctor at the beginning of 2006. West Los Angeles is a center for fertility specialists, and we got several references for a widely respected doctor. Marisa made her appointments and began to see him. She told him on her first visit, "I need you to put me on Clomid." Marisa never went to medical school, but she had talked to her girlfriends and self-diagnosed, and she told him her prescription on the first visit. Being a little more methodical, he ran lots of tests on Marisa and looked at the numbers.

I talked with Jeff about his experience with fertility treatments. "Yeah, it is really all about the egg. There is just one test for us guys, and if the swimmers are swimming, you just have to wait while they find out what's happening with the eggs."

My test was simple, something I had practiced since being a teenager. I didn't even visit the doctor. They just sent me to a lab and the only challenging part was taking my little brown paper bag and specimen cup to a room past the chatting nurses who all paused just long enough for me to think, *They know exactly what I am about to go and do.*

"Here, honey. This is your room. There's a lock on the door and some movies for the DVD. There are some tissues if you need them." My nurse left after giving me those simple instructions. I was curious about the DVD. Turns out this lab thought that a Japanese porno film would be effective, but all I saw were small, skinny actresses putting mousetraps on their nipples. It was one more strange moment in Los Angeles and not at all useful for the task at hand. I turned off the DVD and settled for my imagination.

I spent that week wondering what would happen if my body had a problem. What would Marisa think? How would I feel? But the test results said the swimmers were okay, so I never found out what that would be like. The testing shifted to Marisa and the eggs.

The subject of adoption had come up, and we were considering it. My cousin Joel and his wife Marianna had adopted twice, so I called them to talk about their experience. Jeff and Pam had adopted twice too and we listened to their experiences.

One Saturday night, Marisa and I went to San Diego to see a play. We were driving back to Los Angeles Sunday morning through Camp Pendleton, when I reached Jeff and we talked on speakerphone.

"Yeah, when we first started, I thought it might be something hard," he said. "But you take these adoption classes and you learn about what it's going to be like. Nothing happens quickly—you have plenty of time to adjust. I tell you Dylan, when you finally hold your baby in your arms, even though you've adopted, it's the most natural thing in the world. You just know it is supposed to be. When Pam and I finished adopting Alexandra, it was the most perfect thing. Same way with Jacob." Jeff and Pam had gone all the way to Russia twice to create their family. They had gone through the *in vitro* efforts for several years and a lot of money but finally had gone with adoption.

My cousin Joel, my tall, funny, charismatic, rock-climbing, guitar-playing cousin Joel, had lived north of Los Angeles in a town called Ojai when I first moved to Los Angeles. He was a teacher at a boarding school. He and his wife Marianna adopted twice, bringing home Jasper and Mateo, who are both of African American descent. Joel and Marianna could have had their own children biologically, but they chose to adopt for personal reasons about making a difference in the world.

"It's true what they tell you," Joel said. "The moment you hold your new baby in your arms, he or she is yours. All the connections of parenthood are instantly present. When I held Jasper the first time, and our case worker announced that we were his parents, it was all there, all the love, and all the responsibility, everything."

I was curious and asked Joel what it was like adopting African-American sons when he is Napoleon Dynamite white.

"I think it will matter more when the boys get older. We want them to feel connected to their heritage. We only notice it now out in public, in restaurants, where people stare. You don't realize your white-person anonymity, the ability to go through middle America and just blend in, until you adopt bi-racially."

At our church, we learned about CASA, a Los Angeles institution that works with adoption and foster care. We got all the literature and heard their talk about the processes of getting certified and approved, and onto waiting lists to become adopting parents. They said they have to certify your house too, to make sure it is safe for your adopted kids. I started to despair that we would have to replace all the old, non-safety glass windows in our home. If *in vitro* didn't break the bank, paying for kid-proofing our home would surely do the job.

I was starting to get my brain and heart around adopting. Jeff and Joel made it seem possible. They are two important people in my life who I respect for different reasons—Jeff my civil engineer Aggie roommate and Joel my free-spirit campfire cousin. What they have in common is that being a daddy is a big deal to each of them. They each told me adoption is good and I believed them. I didn't have a problem with adoption; it was more that I had never really thought about it. I was playing catch up and learning about something really big, really important, and possibly really real for us.

From underneath the thoughts about adopting, another darker thought started to arise, about staying married. *Do I stay married to Marisa if it means that I can never be a biological dad?* That was another harsh frontier thought, like when Old Yeller got rabies, cold and impersonal. I had always imagined being a dad. But what if that could not happen with Marisa? Did we make a mistake getting married in our mid-thirties? Is this the price we pay for putting career in front of children?

I've learned in sobriety to pray, and to focus on today's problems only. Today's problem is getting pregnant. That is what there is to focus on. I knew I loved Marisa. I gave my vow to be her husband. First, we are partners and second, we try to be parents. I didn't dwell on it too long. Jeff stayed with Pam. My dad stayed with my mom, not through this particular challenge but through theirs. I could, too. The what-if thought went away as our marriage continued.

Meanwhile, there were more months of the fertility doctor until finally it was time for both of us to go see him for the talk. Marisa had been there many times, but it was my first visit—my lab test with the Japanese DVD had been elsewhere. He seemed like a nice enough guy, but he didn't make much eye contact.

Marisa knew where the conversation would go. She has friends who are nurses and friends who are mommies. It took him almost the full hour. He drew pictures and made analogies to glasses of wine and gas pedals in cars that still don't make sense to me. Finally, he got to the bottom line.

"Keep trying. You are not sterile, but, you aren't going to have kids on your own. You have less than a 2 per cent chance of getting pregnant. *In vitro* is not an option, because there aren't enough eggs." He paused so we could digest what he was telling us, and then continued. "I can give you the number of a great lawyer for adoption. I can also suggest an egg donor. We could get a blond-haired, blue-eyed college student from Iowa or the Midwest. Adoption is a choice, too. There are certain times of the year that are best—ten months after Prom night, or ten months after graduation…"

Marisa prayed. Not right then in his office, but later. It was not a desperate, God-I'll-die-without-a-baby type of prayer. It was the serene prayer of the already gifted, the already blessed. It was an acceptance prayer for this life, exactly as it is, and exactly as it is not. I knew I was blessed when I married Marisa, and that conviction only deepened, as did my respect for my wife, watching her go through this difficult time.

We talked a lot, Marisa and I. Her body didn't have many eggs left. That was the problem. All the plumbing was working, but there were very few eggs. Since *in vitro* works by taking an egg out of the woman's ovaries, fertilizing it, and placing it back inside, we were out of luck because there just weren't the eggs to be found.

Marisa's mom and my mom had five and three kids, respectively, but they had those kids in their 20s, not their late 30s. We talked with our moms and learned that Marisa's mom went into menopause in her early 40s after she had her healthy five children. When the fertility doctor found this information out, it was the deal breaker. He'd looked at the numbers, knowing about Marisa's mom, and came to his conclusion that we had less than a 2 per cent chance of natural pregnancy.

Marisa was somehow serene through it all. She didn't want an egg donor, even if we got a blond-haired and blue-eyed one. She didn't want to carry an embryo that wasn't hers. She was open to adoption. I didn't know what to think. Part of me always assumes my life will go like my parents. They went to college. I went to college. They got married. I got married. They had biological babies. *What will I do?*

I am coming to see the difference between making a baby and being a parent. I am getting clear on two things. I'm clear I love Marisa and want to live my life with her. If our bodies won't make a baby together, that doesn't mean we won't be parents. So I'm clear about my marriage.

I'm also getting clear that it is parenthood I am committed to—not the *kind* of parenthood. Of course I want to see the baby Marisa and I would make. I'm curious and vain and wondering about boy or girl, hair, eyes, skin, smile. My parents talked about how they see themselves in us, my sister, brother and me. I assumed I would do the same someday. But more important than seeing biology play itself out, my mom and dad devoted a major part of their life to being parents. I am getting clear that there is still the possibility of being parents in our future, no matter what the biology says.

We keep trying. We buy more ovulation kits. A 2 per cent chance is still better than zero. Recreation sex or procreation sex, both are still fun, like that bumper sticker, "A bad day fishing beats a good day working." It's like that. Marisa is still an executive. She still travels a lot. Sometimes between the travel and the ovulation kit, the windows are short, and foreplay takes on a pretty unromantic tone.

"You. Here. Now. Turn off the TV," she says.

I tease her, "Is this New Jersey foreplay?"

Marisa's cycle is never predictable. She keeps spending money on the ovulation indicator kits and we keep trying. I'm having a big year at UCLA, with extra admission director duties, and I focus on work to stay distracted.

Nothing is happening, and then fate steps in. Marisa makes one last visit to the fertility doctor. As she is signing out, she chats with the nurse there, Christy.

"Have you tried Chinese medicine?" Christy asks casually. "There's a different doctor who shares this suite in the afternoons. Her name is Dr. Wilson. She's American, but she spent five years in China studying Chinese medicine. A lot of people swear by her."

Christy knows Marisa's case from all the visits. Marisa, prayerful in private, has been positive in public this whole time. Marisa is outgoing anyway, but when she's "on" she is especially magnetic. She draws people to her and they want to help. Christy wants to help.

Marisa and I talk but there is not too much to discuss. If the Chinese medicine is safe and it can help then why not? Maybe I have lived in California too long or maybe we're just hoping for a miracle.

Marisa starts seeing Dr. Wilson, and the reports that come back give me hope.

"Dr. Wilson says in Chinese medicine there are lots of reasons for infertility, and also there are lots of things to do about it," Marisa says. "Chinese doctors refer to something called *cold womb*, and so we are going to warm up my womb. No more ice in my drinks. Warm protein with every meal. No more yogurt. She says American women are addicted to yogurt, but that it doesn't help with getting pregnant. No more jogging, only gentle walking. And travel. I have to cut back on my travel." Marisa paused, and I could hear her not wanting to get her hopes up, but still excited as she continued on.

"She says I have to treat my body with the same tender care I would if I were pregnant. I have to do that before I can get pregnant. She gave me all these vitamins to take. She'll do acupuncture treatments on me. She says the first thing we're going to do is get my menstrual cycle consistent. I said, 'You can do that?' and she said, 'Yes, we can.' Dylan, I've never been consistent my whole life."

So here we go on a new chapter, but at least it is a positive one. If Western medicine can't help us, let's see what China has to offer. We get everything else from China; why not borrow some of their wisdom too, if it will help? Marisa is still optimistic. She would be a great marathon runner. She doesn't quit.

DADDY DIARIES ~

FORTY ONE WEEKS

Dear Baby — October 27, 2006

Dear tiny baby, sleeping inside your mommy,

It's 11:45 on a Friday night in Culver City, California, and I can't sleep. Usually I'm asleep in minutes, but not tonight. I'm awake tonight, thinking about seeing you today for the first time and being your daddy. You were black and white and grainy, but it was you we saw today.

We had our first visit with Dr. Mary Kerr. She's probably younger than your mom and me, and she is special. Your mommy found Dr. Kerr through a nurse named Christy, the same person who recommended Dr. Wilson, the Chinese medicine doctor who helped us get pregnant. We owe Christy a lot.

We sat in the exam room, your mom in a terrycloth robe, while Dr. Kerr asked us lots of questions about how things have been going and what we have done so far. She seemed to have all the time in the world to give us, and our whole visit with her was two hours long. I had never spent two hours with a doctor before. Your mommy was so calm and centered and peaceful when we were finished.

After all the questions, Dr. Kerr put a clear jelly on your mommy's tummy and took your picture using ultrasound. The machine was made by Siemens, the German company where your daddy worked for six years before

UCLA. Dr. Kerr turned on the ultrasound and moved the wand over your mommy's belly, up and down and left and right.

"What a big baby we are seeing! I don't know if I can fit all of this baby on the screen. How far along do you think you are again?" she asked, as she made some adjustments. We still don't know if you are a "him" or a "her" yet.

"Look right there. See the curve? That's the head. And this is a leg," she said pointing to the screen and moving the wand some more. "There is the stomach, that little black dot. We've got a big baby on our hands here mommy and daddy."

You seemed to wave at us. You had a bridge on your nose. We could see the little dot of the fluid in your stomach. You were drinking, which Dr. Kerr told us is a good sign. Your head was big, and we were grateful as she said that a big head is a good sign, too. She measured your leg bone and your head circumference and your length. She determined that you are much older than we had thought. She told us our due date is April 21, 2007, and on the drive home I realized this was Aggie Muster, a good omen.

On the screen, you were a bunch of grainy black and white images, but you were baby-shaped. I stared the whole time, my eyes going from your mommy's tummy to the monitor back and forth.

Then our doctor did the most amazing thing. She flipped a switch on her Siemens machine and there was sound. *Boom-Bwomp, Boom-Bwomp, Boom-Bwomp.* Your heartbeat filled the exam room and I gasped in a gulp of air. My eyes filled with water, and it hit me that you are you and that you are alive. Before that moment, it still wasn't real. We had been trying to have you, but it hadn't been working out. I'd been worried since before we got pregnant, worried whether you'd ever spark at all. But there you were, and your heart is beating.

Nine weeks ago tonight, on August 25, your mommy told me that she had you growing inside her. We went to eat dinner at an Italian restaurant called Maria's. It is on Pico Boulevard in West Los Angeles, across the street from a mall. Maria's has rich meals and we save it for special occasions. I didn't know why but that night I felt like celebrating. It was actually a regular Friday night, but I told your Mommy, "Tonight feels like a celebration dinner."

What I didn't know was that your Mommy did have news worth celebrating. She knew she was pregnant with you, but she didn't share that yet. Instead, she played along and listened to my theory about why I thought today deserved celebration. I said I was in a good mood, and I didn't know why but why not celebrate.

We ate our heavy, delicious Italian meal. Mommy ordered her favorite eggplant parmesan. I had chicken parmesan, which I have learned to order when mommy orders eggplant. If I order anything else, mommy's meal always looks better than mine, and I get jealous. Chicken parmesan always looks good sitting on top of a big bed of sauce smothered spaghetti. We love Maria's because they serve decadent garlic knots dripping with butter. The garlic is so strong it lasts into the next day, but it is delicious. We ate and talked and held hands and were acting silly by the end of the meal, as the carbohydrates kicked in and we were feeling the rush. We loaded up our leftovers in the silver metal tins and brought our big bellies home.

We sat in a happy food coma on mommy's white couch with the alternating pale green and blue stripes, right over there in our living room with the big bay window that looks out at the park. Your mommy took my hand in her hand and looked me in the eye with a smile on her face.

"I want to tell you a story," she started saying. This was different. Mommy doesn't usually do that. Mommy is a Jersey gal, and usually when she wants to say something, she says it. I roused myself from my stupor and sat up to pay attention. I thought maybe she got a new sweater.

"Once upon a time, there was a man and a woman. For a long time they wanted to have a family. They wanted to get pregnant and have a family. And they did get pregnant. I am pregnant, Dylan."

She told the story with my hand in hers. She took a breath before she started and then told it straight to its conclusion. She told it with a smile and a slight downturn of her head. My strong, powerful executive wife was soft and gentle, like a little girl bringing flowers from a field and presenting them quietly. When she was done, I looked at her closely.

"Really?" I asked.

"Really," she answered. "We. Are. Really. Pregnant… Really!"

I felt the happy tears begin to fill my eyes. My food coma was gone, replaced by the moment's newness. We had been trying, and we had been waiting, and we had been trying, and now it was here. I didn't know what to say or do. But I remembered to thank God. I remembered to breathe and smile and to kiss my wife.

"Thank you, my bride. Thank you for marrying me," I said, looking into her eyes. It was kind of a silly thing to say, but it's what I say to your mommy. I love to call her *my bride*, even though we've been married three years now. It makes me feel like we are brand new when I say it.

Good night little baby. Sleep softly tonight.

Love,

Your Daddy

The Day After (Dear Baby, Part 2) — Oct 28, 2006

It's now the day after, and it's all begun to hit me: the many things that would change, the many things that could go wrong, the many things that would be different and beyond my control. It got scary quickly, and I had to stop thinking. In sobriety I've learned, *those are not today's problems*, and they might never come to pass anyway. What is here is you. You are really inside your mommy, your heart is really beating and that is all there is for now.

Son or daughter, I don't know which you are yet, I've learned that what I put out into life, life gives back to me. I call it several things— "creating," or "intending," or sometimes prayer. I call it different things on different days, but putting something out into life is the basis for how I live. I believe life doesn't happen accidentally. I put out the call or the vision, and then I have to get out of bed and go do the legwork to make it happen.

For you, our unborn child, I am a bit challenged as to how to apply all this so that you arrive here healthy, perfect. My mind says to set an intention that a healthy baby is born, or take a stand and visualize the perfect pregnancy, or pray for God to bless this unborn child. This is what I believe I need to do to make sure you come to us healthy and happy. But my superstitions, they say something else entirely. They say, *Be careful.* They say, *Don't get ahead of yourself.* They say, *Don't mess with God. If He wants you to have this baby, you better lay low and let it happen.*

Getting pregnant, and really having the baby this time, seems overwhelming. I want you more than anything. It's not rational, this wanting. It's much deeper than that. But I'm scared if I want you too much, I might make God mad, and then something could change. It's really a lack of faith on my part, like a strange superstition, *Step on a crack, piss off God.*

When I was a kid, in the heat of the summer, my family would drive across the Texas panhandle up to cool Colorado and go camping. I loved the drive and the mountains and the adventure, but the thing I loved most was the fishing. I would dream about fishing before the trip. We'd buy our supplies in the small town sporting goods store, licenses and lures and fish identification fliers. I had a knife and a leather sheath, and I felt like Davy Crockett—a real mountain man. Before we arrived, I'd imagine all the adventures I was going to have, sloshing around the creeks and beaver dams just outside of the campgrounds.

I would also tell myself every time before the actual fishing began: *I'm not going to catch anything.* It was my superstition. It was silly, but I did it every time. I didn't want to get my feelings hurt, and I didn't want to spoil the magic of fishing if I didn't catch any fish. This was the perfect superstition. *Set the expectations low, so there's no way to be disappointed.* And if I happened to catch any fish, well, it would be a bonus.

Now here I am with your mommy. She is pregnant and we saw your tiny little body on the ultrasound yesterday. We heard the Boom-Bwomp of your beating heart. This is bigger than any fishing trip, and I'm more afraid of being disappointed than ever. My superstition is telling me to be careful, to not get too far ahead of myself, because if I do…...

Mommy getting pregnant is a gift. You are a gift. But what if I don't deserve you? I haven't earned this. I've doubted and worried and whined. Your mother is doing all the real work. Sure, she will share credit with me – your mother is a unique and generous human being – but really, it's her who is doing all the heavy lifting.

She willingly changed herself to make this pregnancy happen. She worked at it. She went to an American doctor and took his advice, all the way to the end, when he said we had less than a 2 per cent chance to have a baby. But mommy didn't give up. She found a different doctor, a Chinese doctor, who said, "In our medicine, there are lots of reasons people aren't pregnant, and there are lots of things you can do to still get pregnant."

Your mommy did those things. She ate differently, she slept differently, she changed her job activities, got acupuncture and prayed.

You are 15 weeks old today. We don't know if you are a girl or a boy yet. Before yesterday, we didn't know how old you actually were. We thought you were younger. We haven't told anyone, not your grandparents, nor your aunts, uncles and cousins yet. You've been our special secret for nine weeks. We were waiting to get through the first trimester and before yesterday, we thought we still had a couple of weeks to go.

You have already been on national TV. Last month, your grandma Stafford was visiting, and some of my graduate students at UCLA got tickets for a group of us to go see the television show, *The Price is Right*. We asked your grandma if she wanted to go, and she said yes. If you get a group of at least 20 to go to the taping, they guarantee that one of your group will get called up.

Our whole group was seated in the back corner of the audience but just before taping they came and asked a couple of us to come and fill in empty seats. Your grandma got to fill in the aisle seat of the front row. When Bob Barker came strolling down the aisle, he stopped and shook your grandma's hand—her Hollywood moment.

"What was that like," I asked her afterwards, "when you shook his hand?"

"It was cold and felt like lotion," she said, not particularly star struck.

In the second half of the taping, in the third round, one of the UCLA students got called. "You're the next contestant on *The Price is Right…*" the announcement came. Not only did he get called, but he ended up winning the showcase showdown, the big finale of the show, and they let our whole group go up on stage as the credits rolled. You were on national TV inside your mommy, jumping around next to Grandma. The tricky thing was that we hadn't told Grandma yet. You were still our tiny secret.

Now that we know your age, we are going to tell your grandparents next weekend that Mommy is pregnant with you. Your mommy's parents will be here in person, visiting us on a layover to Hawaii. After that, we will get to tell your other grandparents, my mom and dad.

****

You are from love. That's all I want you to know. It doesn't mean you're better or worse than other kids. It just means that God's presence in your life is maybe easier to see. Doctor Mary Kerr said to us yesterday, "This is a lucky baby. You want to be parents. You have been waiting for this baby. It's not always like that."

I tried to go to sleep last night, but I couldn't. I was a little numb, now that it's all settling in and the initial euphoria is over. It's almost too much for me. My mind wants to short circuit somehow, to fast forward to April 21 and the end of these 40 weeks. And I also don't want to fast forward. I want to savor each day, to remember the chapters we go through, and to appreciate that we didn't always know how much you would bless our lives.

Something more I want to share with you about faith. The week before we found out your mommy was pregnant, I called the Catholic Church and signed up for the RCIA (Rite of Catholic Initiation in Adults) program. It was a little lifting on my part. I was saying to life that I'm ready to be a daddy. I was praying and intending, and this was the step I took to create one common faith conversation in which to raise our future family, the family that you are being born into.

I grew up a Presbyterian preacher's kid, and I was always proud of my denomination. But, just as your mommy had to let go of having to be a mommy, in order to have you, I had to let go of something, too. I chose to let go of one way of looking at God to try on a new way to look at God. That is how it lives for me, letting go to let something new happen, which includes your mommy getting pregnant.

My mom, your Grandma Stafford, is Presbyterian, but ironically she introduced me to a Catholic Priest who ultimately made it possible for me to consider conversion. Two years ago, when Grandma heard Father Richard Rohr lecture in Dallas, she was so impressed with him that she sent me his CD. Since then I've listened to over ten of his CDs, multiple times each, and after I digested them all, the idea of converting to Catholicism seemed natural, even easy. In fact, Father Rohr was speaking in Pasadena this year, and that is why your Grandma Stafford was in town when you got to be on *The Price is Right* with her.

When I was contemplating converting to Catholicism, I called my dad, your Grandpa Stafford, the Presbyterian minister in the family, to ask him what he thought about me changing denominations. He told me, "Son, your first commitment is to your wife now. If you think this will support your marriage, then you should do it."

I asked my dad a question I'd long wondered about, "How come we're Presbyterian anyway, since your dad was Episcopalian and your mom was a Southern Baptist?"

"Well, back in the 1940s, my dad drove a lot for work, and the family had only one car. The closest church in Dallas was St. Andrew's Presbyterian, so that's where your grandma took my brother and me."

"So, we're Presbyterian, mostly because you guys could walk there?"

"You could say that." This conversation took a lot of the pressure off the idea of converting. It wasn't like I was turning my back on ten generations of family history. And hearing my dad tell me to put my wife first cleared my thinking, too.

One idea I have learned lately from Father Richard Rohr is that God's presence is all a gift. The divine indwelling of God is in me, and it is all a gift. I didn't earn it. It is also in your mommy, and it is in you, in everyone, and it is all a gift. God's presence is nothing we earn, even though we mostly think it is. It is gifted to us. Ours is to acknowledge it and receive it—and once we can recognize the divine indwelling in ourselves, we can recognize it in others. That is the bonus idea, that there is the divine in everyone.

In my recovery program, my sponsor Everett taught me that we each have a spiritual plate. God sees how much is on our plate and won't put anything else on it, until we appreciate what is already there. That's how I cultivate the attitude of gratitude, by appreciating what is already sitting on my plate in my life. Recovery has taught me to take on living life one day at a time.

Give us this day our *daily* bread... Not our *weekly* bread. Not our *monthly* bread. Not our *401K* retirement bread.

My precious beloved. You are 15 centimeters long right now. You are curled up asleep inside the woman I love more than anything. It is two days after your mommy's birthday and a few more days after our third wedding anniversary, and you are a gift to us each day, growing inside your mommy. Thank you for coming into our lives.

Amen.

Marisa Moments — November 21, 2006

I've started RCIA, Catholic school I call it, and I am learning the upcoming steps to becoming Catholic. At Easter, I'll get to choose a new name for myself, my confirmation name. That sounded cool to me, and in class tonight I blurted out, "I like *Bono*, the adopted name of Paul, lead singer of the band U2. I want to be named *Bono*." The response was it needs to be a Saint's name. I was disappointed but responded that Bono will probably be sainted someday for his work with Africa and relieving Third World debt. Maybe this could be a pre-emptive saint name? I was told it doesn't work that way.

In her early pregnancy, Marisa was certain we were having a girl. Sometimes she gets hunches, about people or events, and usually they are accurate. A few years earlier, a woman at work who has strong intuitions told Marisa she would have a daughter. It had made an impression on Marisa, and now she felt sure that she was having a girl.

Marisa is from New Jersey. I'm from Texas. She is direct and straight forward like her people from the northeast. I'm kind of pokey and *How ya'll doin?* like my people from the south. When my wife makes up her mind about something, I usually go along with it. *That's mighty fine, mam. Ya'll have a nice day.* Everything works out better when she leads. Marisa seemed like her mind was made up, we were going to have a girl.

Once, before we knew the gender, I was driving to a recovery meeting at lunchtime with the music turned up loud. My best friend Travis had given me the CD *How to Dismantle an Atomic Bomb* by U2 at Thanksgiving the year before—the same Thanksgiving when our first pregnancy had ended. I was blasting the song "Miracle Drug" with the windows down. It has a lyric: *Freedom has a scent, like the top of a newborn baby's head.* Well, that did it. I had one of those *moments*, those beautiful time-stops where everything seems to fit perfectly with everything else. I call them *Marisa Moments*, because for the last few years, such moments almost always have something to do with becoming aware of my love for her.

Travis had been telling me for years that U2 gave the best performance of any group, and he's seen many hundreds of bands. On November 5, 2001, less than a month after 9/11, he got tickets and we drove his convertible Chrysler from Fort Worth to Austin to see U2 in concert. It was his eighth time to see the band, but my first.

We drove down Interstate 35 with the sun setting over west Texas. The drive was glorious, and it was the best show I've ever seen. As much as the music stands on its own, it was U2's connection to the attacks of 9/11 and what they meant for the world that made it so strong. "Even Texas loves New York," Bono proclaimed and the audience roared approval, not like a knee-jerk rock show reply, but like humanity hurting. They played their hit song, "One," while the names of the victims of 9/11 scrolled on the giant stadium monitors. "These are our sisters! These are our brothers!" It was the best moment I'd ever witnessed in rock and roll, these crazy Irish guys coming to the heart of the heartland in a moment of profound pain and saying, *We have all been hurt by this. We are with you.*

That was November 5, 2001. I had only known Marisa six months, since May. We were living in different states and dating long distance. I didn't know she would become my wife. I also didn't know that the next week, I would get laid off from my job of six years with Siemens, not for going to a concert on a Monday night, but because 9/11 crippled the economy and my whole group was let go. I didn't know any of that yet. I only knew a rock band had named my pain and done something to start the healing.

So here I am in 2006, U2 playing on a CD that Travis gave me, tears on my cheeks as I drive down Westwood Boulevard. A flurry of thoughts are hitting me all together, *I'm going to have a newborn baby. I'm going to know what a baby smells like, just like this song. I've seen our baby on the ultrasound. I've heard its heart beating. There is a real baby inside Marisa. We never got this far the other time Marisa was pregnant. That was over so fast.*

I was crying, and I was laughing, and I must have looked like a lunatic. Both hands gripped the steering wheel, and I had to squint to see to drive, but in my mind it was quiet and clear as I thought, *if we have a boy, I would want to name him Bono. Anyone who can write a lyric that beautiful, that makes me feel this way, anyone who tries to make the world a better place like Bono does is a great person.*

I was absolutely focused in my mind, *if we ever have a son, we could name him after an Irish saint-to-be, Bono.*

My dad, Harold Jackson Stafford, Jr. was born in 1943. World War II was going on, and I have to wonder—what were Harold Dear and Bobby Dear doing, making babies? It was two years before the victory in Europe, so Dad didn't qualify as a baby boomer in the wave that came after the war.

Since my dad was Stafford Jr., I could have been a Stafford the Third, but instead, they named me Harold Dylan Stafford. Dylan was Dad's idea. He was an English major and he loved the poems and writing of the Welshman Dylan Thomas. *Rage, rage against the dying of the light,* he wrote and may have inspired Robert Zimmerman to change his name to Bob Dylan.

Thomas drank himself to death early, only 39. I saw his writing shed in Wales in 1994, quiet in the woods and looking out over an estuary, seven years before I realized my own problem with alcohol.

I loved my dad for giving me such a cool name. In traditional Texas, Dylan was unique among the Michaels and Scotts and Lances of my childhood. Older people at church would ask, "Like Marshall Dillon?" I was too young to have seen *Gunsmoke*, but I learned to nod and say "Kinda." The name *Dylan* stood out, and I loved dad for giving me a cool name.

The name's not unique anymore and now I can't go through a mall without hearing some parent somewhere yelling, "Dylan come over here. Dylan sit down. Dylan, don't make me tell your father."

All excited, I called Marisa at her workplace. She knows that this happens to me sometimes, that I get these overwhelming emotional flashes I call *Marisa Moments*. Many times I call her when one is happening and tell her or leave her a gushy message.

She smiled over the phone and asked me, "Would people call him *Bono* like in *Sonny Bono*? Could people in the northeast pronounce it? I guess we could think about it." We were both smiling now. This was my first time to pony up a name for the name game, and besides, choosing a boy's name didn't really mean much, because Marisa's hunch was we were having a girl.

Very shortly after, we went for our second ultrasound. Marisa was on the exam table. Doctor Kerr applied the ultrasound jelly in a happy face on Marisa's tummy. She worked the wand up and down and watched the monitor.

"So, what are your thoughts about knowing the gender?" she asked.

"We'd like to know," we replied. We had talked about it and there would be enough surprises along the way we thought. It would be okay to know the gender now.

"Well, mommy and daddy, you're having a boy. See that right there? That's a boy you've got inside you, mommy." We looked at each other and smiled and held hands. I was misty-eyed as always, but I'm sure I would have been for a girl, too. It took us a long time to get pregnant, and we were told that most likely we couldn't get pregnant, and all that makes this whole experience even more special to me.

Marisa's hunch about the gender was wrong. The second ultrasound told us so. But the hunch about making a family was right on. This was what we signed up for when we got married.

I love my wife Marisa. I love how she laughs and smiles and thinks and talks. I love traveling together and I love going to the movies. I love holidays and regular days. And I can't wait to be parents together.

I've watched my own mom and dad go through lots of chapters as a married couple. They have been role models my whole life, married over 40 years, but what inspires me most is that they still *like* each other. I want to do for our child what my parents so graciously did for me and my brother and sister: be happy parents together for a whole lifetime.

We started playing the name game for a boy. The current options are combinations of our fathers' names, either Jackson Paul or Paul Jackson. I am pulling for a hyphen, as in Jackson-Paul Stafford or Paul-Jackson Stafford. The U2 *Marisa Moment* started the conversations that led to the suggestion of *Bonaventure* as a third name. There really was a Saint Bonaventure and there really is a Bono. It would be an homage to both of them and a hope for a *great adventure*, the literal meaning of the name, with our son.

Having a baby is our next chapter in the adventure of how to be grownups. We paid attention to Open Enrollment in choosing our insurance option this year. Instead of asking which one's the cheapest, we read all the details and tried to decode everything. My long-ignored retirement accounts are getting more attention. I was promised a raise at work, and I started doing the paperwork I'd been ignoring, which will help push it through human resources.

Being married to Marisa is changing. I am trying to manage my tendency to whine and complain differently. Instead of dumping every fear or random thought on her, I'm talking to other people in my life, my father and mother and sister and sponsor, to clean up my side of the street. Then when I'm with Marisa, I can be more focused on what she needs. I want to have something better to share with her than my worry.

Today's *Marisa Moment* was sharing something better. We're having a boy.

Thanksgiving Blues — November 26, 2006

Sunday evening and it's been a perfect Thanksgiving weekend, my 37th. My wife is pregnant. My job is cool. Texas A&M and the Dallas Cowboys *both* won their football games this weekend. They haven't both won on Thanksgiving weekend for seven years. After that football dry spell, I should be happy to the core.

But I'm not.

I went to Catholic Church tonight. I call it church, but they call it Mass. Since I grew up Presbyterian, it will always be church to me. I'm almost ready to begin my conversion to Catholicism. Everything is in place, except that I don't see any value in converting. I sit in church and try to get some nourishment, or at least not judge it too harshly. Clang-y music. Pious readers. People-watching pageantry. I was irritated and judging plenty tonight. *What is wrong with me? Why can't I experience it? Just be, and let the Goodness of God wash over me?*

In the movie *Borat,* when Sacha Baron Cohen as a fictitious Kazakh journalist goes into a Pentecostal revival tent and gets on line to be healed, I was actually moved. He was faking it, but the churchgoers were not—their reaction was real. They didn't know it was a farce and that they were being made fun of. He claimed to have pain, and they treated him with compassion. They gave him the best they had—*their* Jesus. Maybe that's the problem with

Catholicism for me right now. Instead of giving, I'm looking for what I can get. If this is truly the Good News, then *who am I sharing it with?*

****

We did help some people on Wednesday, the day before Thanksgiving. We volunteered to feed the homeless and the needy at a dinner provided by our parish in Santa Monica. Altogether 180 turkeys were served with all the fixings. Marisa and I were assigned to the kitchen, stripping dark meat off the bones. Sitting here now, Sunday evening, last Wednesday seems so far away. Thanksgiving weekends have always been like that for me—long and full.

But Wednesday didn't exactly go right. Marisa and I planned that she would pick me up from work, and we'd go to the church together. Usually I try to leave work early on the Wednesday before Thanksgiving. It feels like a bonus day in the holiday weekend to have those extra few hours. Last year, it rained and we ran errands. Marisa went in to get a honey-baked ham, while I stood in the parking lot with leftover raindrops falling. It had been glorious and cool and perfect.

I wanted that cool and perfect experience this year again, but I didn't get it. My computer froze as I was trying to power down. Marisa was early and waiting outside, but I couldn't turn off the computer or it would mess it up. So I had to stand there looking at my semi-frozen computer, feeling very un-thankful, making us late.

We got to the church, checked in, and got nametags. They pointed us to the kitchen. Had there been an orientation? Had we missed it? The kitchen was too full of people, and I felt grouchy. We were already signed in, and I thought that if we went home now, no one would be the wiser. I thought about proposing this to Marisa but didn't.

I was relieved when Marisa asked me to run her purse back to the car, which I did. But back on the scene, things seemed confused and chaotic. We found someone in charge and got re-assigned to another kitchen in a secondary building. There was more space and fewer people, and this backup kitchen became our home for the day.

Some volunteers had been there since early in the morning. Some were veterans of many years of volunteering. They were genuinely happy to share with us and help us get going. The turkeys came in the side door, several at a time, freshly cooked and donated by local restaurants. Individual parishioners brought in single birds they'd cooked at home. There were even a few Oops-I-ran-out-of-time drop offs of still-frozen turkeys, their embarrassed owners copping to good intentions but underdone results.

One volunteer ran the electric carving knife and made pretty pans of white meat. I donned thin disposable plastic gloves and ripped messy strands of dark meat from legs, chests and backs of turkey carcasses. My sweater was a problem. I'd changed into blue jeans when I took the purse back to the car, but I was still wearing a thin, long sleeved sweater from work. Underneath my plastic apron, the sleeves began sliding down my arms. I couldn't push them up, because my plastic gloves were covered in turkey grease. Scrunching my elbow along my ribs to inch the sleeves up only worked for so long. Marisa finally rolled up my sleeves, problem solved.

I nibbled bites of turkey as I stripped. Would I be able to eat turkey tomorrow, after all of this? Hunger would help, I reassured myself.

After a few hours we went over to see the people receiving the meal. The auditorium was loud and busy, filled with long picnic tables full of people eating overflowing plates of food. There were Santa Monica's long-term homeless with dreadlocks and army hats. There were families small and quiet, not sure how their luck had gone so wrong. There were some people I couldn't discern, who could either be guests or volunteers.

After the meal, people could go over to another building full of free clothing and toiletry supplies and get what they needed. The organization of the meal and the clothing was impressive. How did they get all the food donated? How did they notify the homeless and downtrodden to come and eat? How did they know enough volunteers would show up? It seemed both disorganized and highly functioning all at the same time. It was a faith exercise from my point of view.

My grouchiness went away as I watched the people eating, but I still felt useless. Over-qualified in my mind, thinking I should have helped in the pre-organizing, but under-contributing in reality, since I'm not the best turkey-stripper.

An African-American mom was helping out with her three daughters. They worked with a local shelter, and they were boxing leftover food from our event to take to another meal tomorrow, when I'd be home on the couch watching my Dallas Cowboys. The daughters and I were standing around a table assembling banker's boxes to load the food. The boxes were hard to figure out. Lots of tab A into slot B directions to assemble a box. The middle daughter was near me and struggling. I showed her how to put her banker's box together. Being across the table, my instructions were upside down and backwards, so it took a while, but she got it. Her smile at her first completed box was a highlight of the day. She was proud of her box, and I was reminded that I was here to contribute.

I hope the families and the homeless people were fortified from all the turkey and trimmings. I was nourished by seeing their gratitude and by helping a girl assemble a banker's box. A little bit of *thanks* and a little bit of *giving* for Thanksgiving weekend, maybe I'm getting the hang of Catholicism after all.

Flickers and Flutters — December 8, 2006

I'm here in the dining room in a sweatshirt, jeans and slippers. My half cup of coffee is cool to the point where it barely gives off any steam. I'm looking at an ultrasound photo of our unborn baby. It's either creepy, this photograph from inside the womb, or it's the most beautiful thing I've ever seen. They call the photo "4-D." I'm not sure what the 4 is all about. It looks 3-D to me, but maybe I need some special glasses to see it properly.

"He's got your nose! He's got your lips!" Marisa exclaimed when we saw the 4-D image on the screen for the first time in the doctor's office.

"Hey, paparazzi, bug off," our baby seemed to say, as his little arm appeared to rise up and cover his face and his head tilted inward against the warmth of the placenta wall, away from the intruding ultrasound.

Our baby is only 20 weeks and 2 days old, just over half way done, in the photos taken earlier this week. He's estimated to be 13 ounces. Not nearly ready to come out. Not yet viable even with the top preemie care. And yet for all of that, it's him. I see the little person he is. He's not alien-like, he's baby-like. There are ten fingers and ten toes, one tummy and a big head. He's all curled up and sleeping, eyes closed and warm.

In all the 4-D photos of our baby, I keep looking at the lips. They look like the lips I've seen reflected back at me in the mirror my whole life—*my lips,* identifiable because they are very distinct. I have a wonderful cousin who is sure we have some African in our background. "White people don't have these lips," she swears.

There were two mothers in the doctor's office lobby when we were leaving after our ultrasound. One of them commented, "You'll be amazed when your baby comes and you hold up the ultrasound photo next to him. It really is a photograph. There's no mistaking it."

So, with the magic of ultrasound, we can see his little face and his little body developing. But what about his soul? When does his little soul develop? When does his soul get connected to his body?

It's Christmas time as I write this. Marisa and I watched our DVD of *It's a Wonderful Life* last weekend. We snoozed through the middle, because we had a fireplace and a couch and a blanket, but we did see the beginning, where the stars in the heavens are flickering and the angels are talking to each other. They're deciding to send Clarence, an angel second class, on his mission to earn his wings. He's going to save Jimmy Stewart Bailey by showing him how important his life is to other people.

As I wonder about the soul of our little unborn son, I have an image of his soul out there flickering and waiting and watching its new body developing. It's getting ready to move in to its new home. Or maybe the soul has already moved in? Maybe it happened at conception—*Bam*, all at once—a microcosm of the Big Bang. Or maybe moving in is more pedestrian, like when I moved after college, and my truck was too small, so it took a lot of trips back and forth, and things got broken or forgotten or rained on. Maybe the soul is standing in its 13-ounce-new-home right now, trying to remember which box has the alarm clock inside, or the toothbrush, or the saline solution.

Marisa hasn't felt him kick yet. Our mother-friends call the first sensations *flutters*. "You'll feel the flutters," they tell us. I assumed the flutters were the pre-kicking of a little baby developing. Now I'm thinking that maybe the flutters are really the soul moving in to the body – scooching furniture; hanging pictures; dropping things; looking around with hands on hips saying things like, "Maybe that wall needs a new coat of paint." All those activities of a soul making itself comfortable in its human habitat could feel like flutters, I suppose.

The whole thing is magical, the pregnancy and the growth of the baby in the womb. Even bad people start out in the womb, but I can't believe that they're bad when they're in the womb. Everyone has to have started out holy. But then how does this magic get lost? Well, if I could lose my wallet (which I did this summer), something very tangible and necessary, so I guess I could lose magic, something ephemeral and optional.

Mel Gibson has a new movie out this month about the ancient Mayan culture, *Apocalypto*. Two months ago, I was on top of the same Mayan pyramid that is shown on the cover of Gibson's movie posters. We were in Campeche, Mexico for Humberto's wedding. Seven Texas Aggies, all in our late 30s, huffed and puffed our way to the top of the Mayan pyramid called Edzna. Jeff, Dylan, Brady, Joel, Sean and John, formerly of Bula, Texas, near Muleshoe, were on hand to be groomsmen for Humberto, just as our upperclassmen had predicted we would 19 years earlier, back at Texas A&M in the fall of 1987.

We caught our breath and took digital photos as we paid our own homage to all things primitive. We did something called a *hump it*, which is a special college yell we do at A&M. When we were freshmen in the Corps, if any upperclassmen asked you, "Fish Jones, what outfit are you in?" you had to immediately drop everything, lean forward with your hands on your thighs, and yell the name of your outfit in cadence at the top of your lungs. Any of your other freshmen buddies nearby would drop whatever they were doing and join in. There were different hump it yells for each outfit and one for the whole Corps.

At the top of Edzna, Jeff bellowed at Humberto, "Fish Jones, what Corps are you in?" All of us joined in as loud as we could yell in cadence,

"The Fightin' Texas Aggie Cadet Corps!

The 12th Man!

The Spirit of Aggieland!

The best damn outfit anywhere!

Whoop!"

Our voices echoed out into the jungle, scaring all the iguanas and warding off any evil University of Texas spirits that might have been floating around. The 360 degree view of the jungle showed green in every direction. A thousand years ago, if you saw this view, it meant you were about to be sacrificed. There was scary magic at the top. Good people or bad, I could feel the magic that those Mayan people lived inside. I couldn't help but feel it. We were clearly not in our time, standing on top of that pyramid. Different people built this—different history, different language, different ideas, and different values.

What would it be like to be Mayan, to live in a jungle without electricity? When it got dark, there would be pumas and wild pigs and poisonous insects and snakes. You'd have to be careful of all of those. Plus, you'd have to pay attention since you lived in a society that would sacrifice its sons and daughters periodically to appease the gods. Good thing we've moved past sacrificing our sons and daughters when we get scared.

Magic would be very easy, it seems. The borders would be blurry between what *is* and what *isn't*. If you sat around a campfire, and the older people told stories of dragons and witches and demons and goblins, how would you know if they were telling the truth or not? Wouldn't you wonder what made all those jungle noises outside your tent each night? How would you be able to verify those creatures did or didn't exist?

70

Since we have science today, and we've explored every inch of the world, and we know so much, it seems as if the magic in life has been pushed out of the way. In the new *King Kong* movie, I had to let my imagination say okay when they talked about the undiscovered island. There aren't any undiscovered islands anymore. We've got the satellite images on Google Earth to prove it, don't we?

But back then, there would have been a lot more room for magic. Or, if you prefer, there would have been a lot more room for the holy. In Catholic school right now, we're talking about the Trinity and the Holy Ghost. I like this Holy Ghost. I think he's a righteous dude. He's off to the side, out of the limelight, and away from the paparazzi. He's like the other guy in your favorite band, whose name you don't remember. Bono, the Edge and that other guy. Mick Jagger, Keith and what's-his-name.

The Holy Ghost seems to be like a wandering relative, who doesn't really have a permanent address, who crashes with friends and loved ones, but who, when he arrives, is the life of the party, and you wonder how you ever got along without him. Maybe Mr. Holy Spirit is actually the magic? Maybe the Holy Spirit is visiting with the soul of our little baby boy, helping out with the move. Maybe the flutters are coming from his soul and the Holy Spirit sitting around a dinette table. They've had a big day lifting things up stairs. They've unpacked a lamp, and they're surrounded by lots of boxes. They've got take-out Chinese food and a 6-pack. They're talking and laughing, free from it all in that in-between space of moving. No longer really in the old life but peacefully, blessedly not yet in the new life, either.

Just flickers and flutters.

Dallas Cowboys Lost — December 10, 2006

Dear Unborn Son,

Football. Tonight we have to talk about football. This is a really important topic, and I hate to have to burden you with it at such a precious age. But to prepare you for life, I have to explain football.

Tonight, our team, the Dallas Cowboys, was embarrassed at home in a 42-17 loss to the New Orleans Saints. This shouldn't happen in a perfect world, but son, there are challenges in life, and this is one of them. Now and again, your chosen team doesn't win. It can't be avoided. It happens. It happened tonight. It just happened a few minutes ago.

When I was a boy in the 1970s, we would go to my Grandma and Grandpa Stafford's home in Dallas for Thanksgiving, Harold Dear and Bobby Dear we called them. Very often, the Dallas Cowboys would be playing the Washington Redskins on Thanksgiving afternoon. My dad tells me that Harold Dear would get so excited about the game that he would have to step away from the TV. It was too tense at times, too hard on his heart. That's my grandpa, your great-grandpa. Harold Jackson Stafford, was his name. He played center on the Baylor University football team in 1929. We have his old, leather football helmet still, the kind with no facemask.

Bobby Dear would always serve apple juice, goldfish crackers and Milano cookies when we would visit. Harold Dear smoked a pipe and wore leather vests and as a boy my nose was always pressed against his vest when I hugged him. Those tastes and smells can still trigger memories for me of your great grandparents.

The Cowboys either win or lose. And here's what I have observed. When we win, I exhale and think *well, maybe nothing bad is going to happen*. But when we lose, it's a different story. Life seems dark and dangerous. Even though I know that if we win, nothing good automatically happens, if we lose it's an impending-doom kind of feeling.

My dad calls the team the *cardiac Cowboys*. He likes to say, "No lead is too great that it can't be blown in the fourth quarter by the *cardiac Cowboys*."

This is something I want to teach you, how to enjoy the buildup and hype of football and yet still keep it in perspective and enjoy your life. But I'm not sure how to teach you, since I haven't figured it out yet for myself.

For example, now that the game is over and we lost, I'm tense in my chest and thinking about work tomorrow. I got a promotion last summer, right before we found out mommy was pregnant. Instead of just being director of admissions for one MBA program, this year I'm in charge of two MBA programs. It's a great opportunity, but the timing has become awkward with the extra responsibilities, and I'm not sure how to make it all work. Mommy's pregnancy is called *high risk* because we are a little bit older than average and the most important thing right now is taking care of mommy. I worry I may have messed up in accepting the promotion this year.

Sports teach us to go forward when it seems like we should stop. It's said that 80% of life is just showing up. Sports teach us to persevere even though we may not be able to see where we're going. That is one lesson I would like to teach to you, how to show up for life.

I wonder about the future we are creating for you. Our nation's long war in Iraq doesn't seem to have made the world a safer place. We rush around and burn up lots of gas, and I heard today on the radio that thousands of gorillas and chimpanzees are dying from the Ebola virus. Will there be a clean world left for you to play in? Here in Los Angeles, things are awfully crowded and busy.

One thing we have going for us is your mommy. She's a heck of a human being. She is a reminder of everything that can be great about life. You and I, we are very blessed and lucky to have her with us. With mommy, it's not just about surviving; it's about how great life can be. That is a wonderful thing about your mommy. She has a deep reserve of life in her, and she shares it with people and it creates magic.

If it turns out that you don't like sports, son, I will be okay with it. But I imagine you will like sports. My hope is that you see sports as a chance to stretch your body and mind and spirit, while you learn about getting along with other people. There are many lessons that sports can teach. Winning and losing are two. There are many more.

I love you, my son. I hope that you and mommy sleep peacefully through the night tonight. You guys are on a business trip to Florida. Last night, she woke up every two hours because her body had to go to the bathroom a lot. I worry a little bit about her. But, I know that worry won't do any good, so I try to let go of it and cultivate faith.

Good night, my unborn son.

Your dad,

Dylan

Daddy Worries and Dreams — December 11, 2006

If being a parent is such a great thing, then why am I so worried about it? This worry didn't begin when we got pregnant again. No, this worry started earlier, like 15 or 20 years earlier.

In junior high school, while discovering girls, rock and roll, and Dungeons and Dragons, I did some thinking about being a dad. I watched my mother and father struggle through lean years as my dad went back to graduate school full time, and we lived off mom's teaching salary. We had a modest home and drove good if used cars, but things still seemed tight, money-wise.

Money wasn't something my family talked about *out loud*. Were we too proud, too superstitious? Not that our situation was dire or out of our control. My dad was *choosing* to go back to school, studying hard and commuting long hours because he wanted to. But still, money was never discussed *out loud*. That was the killer. Money, or the seeming lack of money, was the only thing we didn't talk about in my family.

There were hints. The silent subject showed up on summer vacations in Colorado, when fishing licenses seemed *a lot more expensive this year*, as did gas for the drive. It showed up when, as a 15 year old, I brought my dad my dream car in the *Auto Trader* magazine—a used Mazda RX-7. He didn't say we couldn't afford it. He said he didn't think it was the car for me. But I was paying more attention to what he didn't say than what he did say.

It showed up Christmas morning. We'd all take longer to open gifts, stretching out the morning to fill the space. Now that sounds spiritual and appreciative, and in a way, it was, but not enough to obscure the elephant in the room. What we weren't talking about almost drowned out the Christmas spirit. After years of this we-don't–talk-about-money atmosphere, my teenage boy brain, trying to make sense of it all, arrived at this formula: *Problem = not enough money; therefore, Solution = enough money.*

I started to pay attention to money in all the places a teenager goes to learn about life: movies, radio, magazines. And I soon realized that there was another problem: People with enough money don't have enough time. And, people with enough time don't have enough money.

This new problem was everywhere. Movies were always showing rich kids emotionally abandoned by super successful career parents, or poor kids whose parents loved them but were too exhausted from work to be available. Radio didn't help. Cat Stevens sang about the little boy blue who's waiting for his career dad, *When you coming home? Son, I don't know when...*

Another formula I was learning: *When = someday = never.* The son grows up and repays his dad by becoming too busy himself. A busy-ness cycle is passed from generation to generation. It was hopelessness-making stuff for me as a teenager. If the adults can't figure it out, and the artists are all telling us about how bad it is, what was I supposed to do?

So here's how I handled my fear about growing up. I told myself to always make the safe choices, the conservative choices. And I *didn't talk about it.* Work hard, hope for the best, and pass along my worry to the next generation. I didn't ask my parents for help. I took the circle of life and spun my own circle of worry.

I chose Texas A&M University not because it inspired my dreams, but because it seemed big and solid and predictable, and my Denison buddy Steve said it was a good choice. I trusted him. A&M actually intimidated me, because it was so big, and I thought it would keep me on the safe path going forward. In high school, as a student body president and National Merit Scholar, I'd had some out-of-state college choices, but they seemed too extravagant—too expensive. So, too, the private, in-state choices like Baylor or Trinity.

Those schools involved student loans or family financial support, subjects that fell into the category of *we don't talk about that*. Nobody ever said overtly, "Don't talk about money for college." It's just what I thought was the right thing to do. I rationalized that since my brother and sister were coming up behind me, the cost of going to college was up to me, and I was on my own. I made this decision silently, never discussing it with any family member.

At Texas A&M, I signed up for Electrical Engineering, the major Steve chose, Steve who was oh-so-much better at math than me. I joined the Corps of Cadets. Could I get more conservative, more practical? I spent high school wearing Van Halen rock-concert t-shirts with the sleeves cut off, and I expected college to involve lots of late nights and cigarettes and great conversations about *the meaning of it all*.

For someone like me, a rock and roll rebel without a clue, Texas A&M + Electrical Engineering + Corps of Cadets was a radically conservative departure. I couldn't see it at the time, but in retrospect it is clear. That was my reverse-deal-with-the-devil. Robert Johnson, the famous blues musician, legendarily stood at the crossroads at midnight and sold his soul to the devil in exchange for the power to play the blues. Instead of standing at the crossroads and bargaining for music and art, I was telling the universe, *I will exchange passion and fun. I will forsake experimentation and wonder. I will sign up for something boring and predictable. As long as you guarantee me that everything turns out okay.*

The funny thing is this. The universe doesn't *want* me to be miserable, to give up passion and creativity. It will, however, let me create my own misery. It will let me go very deep, for as long as I'd like, but intrinsically, the universe isn't *asking* me to be miserable. What they teach us in sobriety is that the illness of alcoholism is like an elevator that only goes one direction, down. The good news is that we can get off the elevator at any time.

In college, I made a deal with myself, to knuckle down and fly right, especially my first year. I lived a cloistered freshman year with Corps activities and not one single date, with all-nighters cramming for 8:00 a.m. chemistry exams and weekends dedicated to supporting the *fightin' Texas Aggie* football team and helping build the Aggie Bonfire. It was fun in its way, but it felt like playing someone else's game.

In my sophomore year, I got a girlfriend and started to make up for my lost weekends. Then, my junior and senior years, alcohol and partying began to dominate my weekends and spill over into part of my week. Too many nights I spent at *The Dixie Chicken*, playing dominoes with Jeff and Brady and Humberto, looking at girls, and enjoying $3 pitchers of beer, moving out too far in the opposite direction from my cloistered freshman year. In my senior year, worry about what comes after college gradually had me looking for *safe* choices again in order to make sure that *everything would turn out okay.*

Fast forward a decade from 1991 when I graduated from Texas A&M to 2001 when I met my wife to-be, Marisa. My good fortune came in threes in 2001.

1. I surrendered. Through the gentle intervention of my mom and sister, my decade-long drinking problem was presented to me in a way I could no longer deny. I gave up the idea that I could drink like a normal person. I turned my will and my life over to the care of a loving God, who removed my desire to drink, and has continued to do so, one day at a time, ever since.

2. I made a commitment to myself and my future. I signed up for a Landmark Education "Wisdom Course" about pursuing your dreams. No ordinary course, it took place on a cruise ship, sailing around the Mediterranean. It was the late-night, conversation-rich, college experience I'd always wanted, that I'd missed at both Texas A&M as an undergrad and the University of Chicago while getting my MBA.

3. I met "the One." During that same course on that same cruise ship, I met and began dating the woman of my dreams, my future wife, Marisa Szem.

All three had to happen for any of them to happen. Without my *slow-briety*, my own one-day-at-a-time reprieve from drinking, I wouldn't have had enough staying power to pursue anything of stature or difficulty in life—career, marriage, parenthood. Without the course about going for my dreams, I'd still be taking all the safe routes, trading off passion in pursuit of security. And most importantly, if I hadn't registered for that course and set foot on that ship, I'd have never met Marisa, who today is not just my wife—she's my angel, my undeserved gift from God.

By the time I met her, Marisa had already been proposed to three times, and she had turned three men down. If I still drank, she wouldn't have noticed me, let alone dated me. I would never have knelt on one knee under that Linden tree and heard her say, "Yes, Dylan, I will marry you."

And what dream am I becoming now, that I am sober and married? I am becoming a writer. I sit. I write. I do the things a writer does. I write crappy first drafts. I set them aside. I come back to them and improve them. I take my humble hat-in-hand and find people to publish them and read them. I am a writer.

I'm named after a poet, Dylan Thomas, an alcoholic one who drank himself to death. Art and expression always seemed too dangerous to me. But sobriety and marriage, and now pregnancy have provided enough stability to re-open the dream I've always had of being a writer. This second pregnancy, which we were told wasn't going to happen, seems like a second chance, and one I must respond to. Now I'm living the dream I used to only think about. I'm not waiting, justifying, getting ready, for *someday*. I'm living this life now. Mommy's making a baby and I'm making my stories.

Buying—Best Left to the Pros — December 12, 2006

Santa Monica, California, Volkswagen service waiting room

As we go through the second trimester watching our unborn baby growing, we are starting to think about the baby's room. In the process, I make a mistake and go to a children's furniture store all by myself, un-chaperoned, without my wife. I walk into *Babyland*, or some such sweet-name for a baby store. Sitting idly at the center command station, two women with we-had-our-kids-a-long-long-time-ago looks on their faces size me up as I stroll about.

"Need any help, love?"

"No thanks. Just looking." I feel guilty, like I'm underage in a liquor store and trying to steal a *Playboy* magazine. No reason to feel this way. I doubt this store even sells *Playboy*.

Of course, I need help. I don't have a clue. But, when I'm clueless, my first reaction is always to get quiet and try to figure it out on my own. It's a pitiful, useless strategy, but it's paid for, so I drive it.

I see the stroller section. There are dainty, old-school models for a walk around Kensington Gardens on a spring English morning. There are aggressive, off-road, knobby-tired California models for the yuppie jogging couple on the go. I note modest price tags under $200, to really crazy price tags—up, up, and away, like everything in Los Angeles.

I felt the same way before our wedding, paranoid and off-kilter. My entire worldview was that mean-spirited people were hovering, about to pounce and take advantage of us, the hapless young lovers. My job was to remain vigilant and prevent being taken advantage of. I accumulated evidence for my worldview. (I always accumulate evidence.) Sure enough, when we lowered the wedding guest count with the caterer, *boom*, the price of the coffee went up.

"Ah ha! Let this be a lesson to all who follow us. Always tell your caterer a low number first. You can always raise it if need be, but you can never, ever lower it."

So, there I am again, in new territory, wandering in baby land and feeling like I could get ripped off at any moment, maybe even mugged by the wrinkly women behind the counter as I stop to innocently look over the 4 ounce and 8 ounce bottles and their matching nipples. Common sense finally takes over. *Get out of here, quick! Run for your life*—and come back with reinforcements, namely Marisa. She'll know what to do. She'll defend me against the evil septuagenarians that are looking to take advantage of my innocence. I leave abruptly.

My next visit to *Babylandia* is completely different. It happened one night when we started out to see a play at Loyola Marymount, but I left my office in such a hurry that I forgot the tickets. When we got to the gate, the guard couldn't figure out where to tell us to go, since I didn't have the event name. We were late anyway, so we gave up and drove through the campus to the other side. But in that random-delicious way life goes sometimes, we got lost leaving the college campus and exited onto a street that had a baby furniture store on it that we couldn't miss.

"Let's go check it out," Marisa chimed.

"Oh, let's," I said, faking a smile and remembering my last such visit. More expensive strollers. More older women at a command center in the middle of the store. But, with my wife on the scene this time, everything else was different. Marisa instantly took charge, going into her New Jersey, unapologetic, you-will-give-us-a-great-bargain mode. She had the women thumbing through catalogs, telling us about color options, explaining special ordering and delivery right to our doorstep. The owner emigrated from Iran a long time ago, and she was loving meeting my wife.

Marisa in action was great to watch. She wasn't fearful. She was fully in control. She was learning as she asked her questions. She was analyzing, giving the owner a chance to showcase her wares.

A short Hispanic woman, very pregnant, stood alongside of us looking at a bed. We started talking. *I like the natural wood. Not me. What's with the plastic covering on the railing? That's because they'll chew on it once they can stand in the crib. Chew on it, like a pet? No, silly, chewing like a child. Ohh... I didn't know they did that.*

The Hispanic woman is pregnant with her second child. She's a wealth of information and shares it in a pleasant way. "If I could afford it, I'd get the transformer crib." *Transformer crib?* A crib that later unfolds and turns into a bed. *Oooh.* Very utilitarian. Daddy-likey-very-much.

Marisa and our co-customer go head-to-head weighing pros and cons. I have a thought about people, and when they give their best in life. This short gal, almost as big around as she is tall, budgeting and gauging on how to bring her second child into the world, could be a $200,000+ a year saleswoman if she were a pharmaceutical representative, or saleswoman of the year if she sold high-end cars. Her knowledge and her passion combine, and I'm in a trance.

"Let's ... let's get what she recommends," I stammer.

Marisa, of course, is still actually in charge. She digests the data but reserves total executive oversight before any actual decisions are going to be made. We make our polite farewells, our brief encounter coming to its natural end.

The owner of the store approaches Marisa about 20 minutes later with yet another catalog in hand to show what can be ordered. The owner makes a suggestion: "Have a seat in the glider. You've sat in a glider before, haven't you?"

No, actually I have not. And, wow, gliders are marvelous things. *Pregnancy? Baby? What baby?* We need one of these gliders for us. I can mount it five feet in front of the TV and watch football for the rest of my life.

Marisa acclimates to her glider seat as a stationary control center. Now she can spread out the various catalogs all around her. She gives me instructions to go forth and verify different details and measurements of the actual floor models that are in the store, cross-referencing my reports to the catalog descriptions.

By this time, I've been in babyland for over an hour. My brain is starting to go numb. I'm reaching the high altitudes of my shopping tolerance. If we were in the Himalayas, I'd be switching over to oxygen very soon. My wife, of course, is a native. She's like the Sherpa guide who only needs a light jacket to hike up a few miles without any need for an oxygen mask.

"Why don't you go gas up the car while I continue looking at the catalogues? Marisa suggests, letting me know she knows that time has come. "When you get back, I'll probably be ready to wrap it up," she says mercifully.

The warden has arrived and returned to me my pre-prison clothes. *Free at last. Free at last. Thank God almighty, I'm free at last.* My wife is savvy about people, and she can read me like a big picture book. I gave it the old college try and went as far as an amateur could ever be expected to go. Now it was time for me to gracefully step aside and let the professionals finish out this session.

I go gas up the car. Blessed man-work. I stand at the pump in the cool California evening. There's a hint of the sunset fading into the western sky. I log the gallons and mileage in my little book. I ponder getting the squeegee and going at the windows but decide against it. They're not *that* dirty, actually.

I loop around the block and get a great parallel spot in front of the baby furniture store. I can actually peer in and see my wife still seated in her temporary glider. She's got the store owner hovering around her, and another new mother has joined the effort.

I pause for a moment, now somewhat revived from the practical job of gassing up the car, before I go back inside.

Fighting Texans — December 13, 2006

In Catholic school this week, they were telling us the punch line to the whole Catholic religion. I like punch lines. They sum up the action, tidy all the loose ends, and leave you laughing.

"Don't Worry."

That's the punch line. They talked about Jesus being born into an occupied area in a time of intense political strife, sort of like Iraq in 1995 during the no-fly-zone era. It was a tough time and people were scared, and Jesus' arrival hearkened in the Good News of peace on earth. *Don't Worry* his arrival communicated, there's more going on than meets the eye.

It got me thinking about my country's war in Iraq. This war started three years ago, six months before our wedding. This war is still going on now, even after a *throw the bums out* mid-term election. This war has cost us the blood of over 2,000 of our soldiers—children of this generation—and we are paying for it with the treasure of my unborn child's next generation.

My dad was born during World War II. I was born during Vietnam and now it looks like our son will be born during wartime too. Four generations back, my grandfather was the last male born during peacetime.

Is this my America now, war without end, amen?

It's tempting to blame, but my former boss in Germany, Lothar, used to say, "Dylan, if you bring me a problem, without a solution, you're still part of the problem." I hated it when he said that. So, what have I done about this war? I've meekly gone along for three years trusting our government. Rationalizing, *Well, if I had the responsibility to protect our nation, could I do any better? Maybe the Patriot Act really is necessary in this new electronic age? Maybe pre-emptive war makes sense? Maybe they weren't really lying about weapons of mass destruction, just misinformed?*

I think about my buddies from Texas A&M who are career military, Brady and John and Chris and Erik and Kevin and Brooks and so many more, whose job it is to execute our government's goals.

Brady and I were roommates at A&M. His nickname in the Corps was *Hack*, because our cold, pre-dawn morning runs made him cough. We ran a lot in the Corps, rain or shine. Our freshman-year dorms hadn't been renovated yet and still had those old-fashioned, mold-growing heaters. We took a lot of Nyquil in the winter months to keep going.

Brady married Melissa. They were from Pearland, Texas, and started dating when she was in eighth grade and he was a high school freshman. They dated all the way through college and then got married. They've had a military career, moving from base to base all over the world and raising three great kids along the way. They got stationed in England and shipped over Brady's big, black Texas pickup truck. Melissa tells funny stories of trying to drive it on streets designed for much smaller cars.

Brady has served our country his whole career, and been a daddy to three kids at the same time. I feel small by comparison, getting ready for one child, going to a desk job at UCLA in Westwood where no one shoots at me.

Even the Dixie Chicks, the all-woman country and western band, had more guts than me. They're fellow Texans. They spoke their mind about our current war, in public, in another country *for goodness sakes*, and took the slings and arrows because of it. People burned their CDs and labeled them unpatriotic and worse. But they exercised their freedom of speech. They exercised one of those freedoms we've shed blood to keep for over 200 years, that my old Aggie roommates have gone to war to protect. The Dixie Chicks reminded me that part of patriotism is standing up and speaking out. We founded this country out of our distrust for tyrannical government, not out of silent obedience.

Fear. Fear. Fear. Yellow. Orange. Red. If we let ourselves stay scared, aren't the terrorists winning? If we really believed this Don't Worry idea would we run our affairs this way?

What will I tell my future son? How will I explain my actions, or my non-actions, about creating the planet he gets to inherit from me?

"Daddy? Did you think that the war on Iraq was a just war?"

"No. Iraq was a sovereign nation not connected to 9/11."

"Then what did you do about it?"

What will I say? I didn't go and fight the war like Brady. I didn't fight against the war like the Dixie Chicks. I went to work at UCLA. I read admission applications. I was faithful to your mommy. I prayed for the soldiers, many of whom are my friends. But was that enough?

Oh, and I started writing. And I'm trying my best not to give up.

I read books about writing, to try to learn how to do it. Stephen King compares the craft of writing to the way his grandfather made cabinets. You need a workshop and space and time and practice. It is a craft. You have to ply your craft. I'm learning the craft of writing.

Stephen likes to tell all those magical tales. I want to tell people how much I love my wife. How grateful I am for her. How my life is better with her. But when I read what I write, I often get self-conscious and think, "Who wants to read about you? Who are you kidding?" Those thoughts make me want to give up.

Stephen King tells the story of how his breakthrough novel, *Carrie*, almost didn't happen. He lost hope and threw the draft in the trash, saying to himself, "What the hell do I know about teenage girls?"

His wife Tabitha found it, pulled it from the trash, smoothed out the papers, flicked off the cigarette ashes and read it.

"You've got something here," she said. "Keep writing the story. I'll help you fill in the part about the teenage girls." Don't worry and don't quit, she counseled her husband and *Carrie* introduced the world to Stephen King.[1]

King makes another point about putting his writing desk in the corner, away from the distractions life. He says that art is a support system for life, not the other way around. My writing desk is out on the porch, out of the way.

Sitting and writing, practicing, is supporting my life. It is lessening my worry about our pregnancy, our war. I'm dusting off my dream of being a writer in honor of our pregnancy. I'm trying to honor my soldier friends' sacrifices and also be an example for my future son. We're free to follow our dreams in America, and the least I can do is follow mine. I'm trying to live by example, to exercise one of the freedoms that make our country worth fighting for.

[1]King, Stephen. *On Writing: a Memoir of the Craft*. New York: Scribner, 2000.

Pregnant Christmas — December 23, 24, 25 2006

Short Hills, New Jersey 11:15pm

We're in New Jersey, Short Hills, and it's 11:15 p.m. We've come back to our hotel room from the first night with family. First holiday greetings are great. Smiles and love—and choices. Handshakes? Hugs? Kisses? I've been in the family several years now, so hugs all around and some kisses, too. Hugging the little ones. Do you bend over or squat? One arm or two? Does anyone else ever think about all of this? And will I get a chance to exercise at all this week? Anything except my jaw muscles, that is. Eating is a major activity.

Tonight I watched my father-in-law Paul, the future grandpa of our baby, make a key lime pie cheesecake with our nephew Connor, his fifth of eight grandkids. How beautiful was that? Connor is one of the sweetest kids I've ever known. He's Marisa's sister Bonnie's second of three children. He's an 8th grader and he loves sports—a magnificent young man.

Grandpa drove 12 hours today, up from South Carolina, leaving at 3:15 a.m. This same man was making key lime cheesecake with his grandson at 9:30 p.m. That was one long, beautiful day and a lot of love between generations.

It's great to have brothers-in-law. Gary is one of mine. He's married to Bonnie. He's an electrician and Connor's dad. Tonight he'd been at Bonnie's business, helping her, and didn't get home until about 20 minutes before we had to leave. He's a loving guy. They have been together for 19 years now. They've got a beautiful home, three great kids, and a dog named Bella.

Gary always makes me feel okay, as if melding into the family isn't that hard and I should just go with it and everything will be fine. He's never said that out loud, and I never really talked about it, but whether he knows it or not, that's how I always feel in his presence, and I appreciate it a lot.

It's great being around both my in-laws since their visit to Los Angeles in November, when Marisa and I let them know that she was pregnant. They're happy. We're happy. It still feels like we're sharing the most wonderful secret, even though everyone knows Marisa is pregnant.

When I was a kid, I never realized that my two sets of grandparents didn't always know each other. I thought they were all friends, and had known each other forever. Now I see that families have to put effort into it. People have to drive and fly and then be gracious at the end of long trips. It doesn't happen without effort.

I appreciate the effort that my father-in-law puts into making a pie with Connor. I hope our future son gets to do that with him too. I appreciate the way Gary has helped me feel at home as the newest son-in-law. I appreciate how Marisa has made it all so seamless.

My beautiful bride is already in bed. I'm going to wrap this up for now. My eyelids are sleepy. She's the heart of it all. She's my connection to this family. This whole experience, marriage and now pregnancy is amazing.

December 24th

It is Sunday morning, the day before Christmas. We did not go to church today. We got up but Marisa was nauseated. She went back to bed. I went to the gym in the hotel and did 30 minutes on the elliptical machine. A small miracle: health during the holidays.

I can see Marisa's belly getting larger and larger. We are at week 23 plus one day. Yesterday, at lunch with Marisa's college friends, we heard of the experiences two of them had getting pregnant and starting their families. One couple used *in vitro* fertilization, having five embryos implanted that developed up to week 21, and then all five aborted. What would that be like, to lose five little babies at once? They held a funeral for all five and sent out cards listing all their names. They tried again however, and this time she was impregnated with three embryos. One embryo fell out, but the other two became their beautiful children. The other mom at lunch had her two children pretty easily, but then she got cancer and had to deal with that. Life, life, life.

I listened to Joel Osteen, a mega preacher from Texas, on the TV in the workout room this morning. My intention was to listen with an open mind, to listen for the good news in his message. He was preaching to an indoor stadium full of people, including black and white people worshipping together, which you don't see much. If I understood him right, his message was about establishing a covenant with God. In the Bible, there are stories of two covenants people have made with God, the Old Testament version and the New. In each story, blood is spilt in the making of the covenant between God and the people, and this covenant is the connection. We are blood brothers with God. Jesus already paid the price, and what we are to do, Osteen said, is take the actions to love, while we live in the knowledge that the debt has already been paid. I thought about the "Don't worry" message of the Gospel that I learned about in Catholic school. I thought about Father Rohr and the divine indwelling idea, that life is all a gift. I wondered if this Texas mega-preacher was offering a different take on those ideas.

Osteen went on to speak of asking for God's power to deal with any challenge that we face, illness, debt, addiction, strife in the home. His message made sense. I heard transformation and recovery and plain old guidance in his words.

What would it be like to get a calling? To hear, as the famous preacher Billy Graham heard, "Go son, and preach the Word of the Lord." How would I respond to that call, or whatever my version of a calling would be? Would I hear it? Would I recognize it? Would I respond?

Osteen preached about not planning for a bad outcome. He said that just because your grandma had diabetes and your mom had diabetes, don't plan on it yourself, don't invite that illness into your future. Where does my incessant worrying fit with that message? He himself has a family history that includes heart disease, but he is not planning on that. He says thank you each night for the health of his body. He asks for strength to deal with making good choices about eating and making sure to exercise.

I loved to hear that. It was personal and applicable and real in a pedestrian, this is what faith might look like on an actual Monday morning, kind of way. I was nourished by his message.

December 25th, 2006—Long Valley, New Jersey 12:05 a.m.

It's after midnight, Christmas night. We are staying at Gary and Bonnie's house tonight. Most of the house is asleep. My father-in-law and brother-in-law are both asleep on the couch with ESPN on the big screen telling us one more time how the AFC and NFC wildcard teams could play out the season.

My wife went to bed about 30 minutes ago. She's crashed on the pullout couch in the room with the Christmas tree and all the presents. I was about to go to bed, teeth all brushed and the day over. But, as I picked through the luggage looking for my sleeping shorts, it occurred to me that this moment was the only quiet I'd get today, and I'm on California time and not tired yet. So why not write?

I married into a big family. I always dreamed about marrying into a big family. My family was medium, and in a grass-is-always-greener-way it seemed like a bigger family would be better somehow, more love and commotion and fun. Well, it is all those things, but it is also big. Big all over. Lots of people, lots of food, lots of conversations, lots of gifts, lots of love. It was not quiet. I have to digest it somehow.

At some moments, I can't really deal with all of it, honestly. I'm attempting to keep a good attitude and give more than I take, but it's overwhelming. There are more kids and more presents in one Christmas than in my total childhood growing up. I wonder what this whole generation of kids will be; who were born in the affluent 90s and raised in these new-generation, 3,000+ square foot homes with so many presents and so much entertainment.

They are generous kids, the ones in this family. They are polite, and give hugs and kisses and appreciation for gifts. They share. They are inspiring. But my mind tells me that all of that isn't possible, that with too many gifts, the kids will be spoiled and selfish. But my theory doesn't hold up when I watch them.

Bonnie and Gary have raised respectful, team-playing little people. They are a model for how I hope we raise our son. They raised their kids out here, in the hills of New Jersey, in a big home with a big yard with no fence. It's a Texas kind of feeling, limitless and open. I never knew New Jersey was like this.

I had three conversations with the three oldest nephews yesterday. My intention was to be interested, to pay attention, ask questions and be generous. The oldest nephew started college two years ago, but isn't attending now, choosing to live with two buddies and work at a retail store. The middle nephew finished a first semester at college, and while he has a lot of complaints about the experience, his grades were solid and he seems to be launched into a good trajectory. The last nephew is a senior in high school and has heard back from some of his college applications and is waiting on others.

I'm overwhelmed by the whole challenge of raising a human being to be a contribution to others and to be true to himself, to family and to society. It seems insurmountable to me, and yet I come from a family of educators. My mother taught for 23 years and my dad works for a school district now. Even my father-in-law was a teacher. They all raised kids who turned out okay, so why do I worry?

There seem to be too many people on the planet to all possibly be taken care of, or so my mind calculates it. The mind calculates, the spirit yearns, and the heart knows what the heart knows. All I have to do right now is get ready to take care of one, the little one growing inside of my wife.

How about me, myself and I? I'm carrying around more fear about my job and future than I realize. Is that why I've got the writing bug? A creative outlet to keep me sane? Maybe. But truthfully, I'm jazzed about this writing genie that's been let out of the bottle.

Maybe I'll become a middle-aged white rapper? Maybe I've got some poetry in me yet. It could be. As I've read other writers and what they think about the craft, I continually hear them state that writing makes life more interesting. I've observed that from writers as diverse as Anne Lamott and Stephen King, and David Sedaris and Frank McCourt.

Being a budding writer this week gave me pause to observe as well as participate. I noticed today, at noon Mass on Christmas day, a few hours after people had eaten huge breakfasts and opened presents that some people didn't look very happy. I saw people with worry and concern on their faces, even though the big celebration just happened and everyone got what they wanted.

Being a still-in-school Catholic, faking my way through all the long prayers everyone else already knows and learning all the genuflecting and crossing, I noticed how Catholics cross themselves in different ways. Some people do the up, down, left right version. Some do it twice. Some thrice. I saw one family, after taking the wafer, who all did a left, right, down and then chin touch move. Never saw that one before. Being a baby Catholic is interesting.

I read my short story I wrote about shopping for baby furniture to my in-laws today. I still get intimidated by my father-in-law Paul and I worried he'd scoff, but he didn't. Everyone was generous and encouraging and it was special, having something artistic to share. It's the best.

Then I thought what kind of life would be possible if I always brought something to share, something precious, something original? I don't know, but it occurs to me like that would be life-transforming. As I was reading my story to my family today, I noticed how I didn't read it 100% literally, how my own natural speaking style influenced how I recreated the mood, subtly trying to improve things.

When am I ever going to have enough time to write, once the baby comes? What if I didn't ever watch football again and used that time being a writer? Probably not happening. One of the writers I'm reading who teaches writing, Anne Lamott, tells about the mighty power of *writing shitty first drafts*. Is that what I'm doing right now? I don't know for sure, but I do know that I promised myself to be a writer, and this is what writers do, they sit and type. I'm trying to honor that promise. I'm also honoring Christmas day. I'm not collapsing, exhausted and full, but rather taking this time to be still and quiet and reflect on this beautiful life I'm living. I am practicing being a writer.

Happy Birthday, baby Jesus. I hope you enjoyed your birthday. Today the priest told us that the season of Christmas doesn't end until January 8th. I hope the entire season is peaceful for you.

Felt the Baby Move, Just Yesterday — December 31, 2006

I love the John Denver song *Back Home Again* with that lyric "Felt the baby move, just yesterday." I actually felt Jack, as we've started calling our unborn son, move for the first time four days ago, on December 27th. That was week 23, plus 4 days. We were still in New Jersey watching a UCLA football game on TV. We were back in our hotel room to give Bonnie and Gary a break. That is one of the perks of Marisa working for a hotel company.

The UCLA Bruins got beat in the Emerald Bowl by Florida State, 27-44. Marisa has noticed that as she gets still, the baby gets active. I lay next to her quietly with my hand on her tummy. After awhile, there it was… *bump*. Nothing in particular about it, just *bump*. Maybe Jack, slated to make his entrance into the world at the UCLA hospital, was stomping mad about the poor showing by the Bruins. But it was there. Motion. Definitely not something that a normal tummy would do. It was the first time I felt it happen.

I wasn't as overjoyed as I have been at other milestones, like finding out Marisa was pregnant at the beginning and hearing the boom-bwomp heartbeat at the first ultrasound. *Everything can't be a peak experience* is how we say it in recovery. *We can't be happy all the time.* So, with that acceptance, it's okay that I'm just regular happy.

I've been sick the last three days, since we came home from Christmas in New Jersey with Marisa's family. It's a chest thing that's got me. Drinking lots of liquids. Lots of sleeping and a good bit of TV football therapy.

Marisa is running errands this afternoon. I ventured outside for the first time in the three days I've been sick. I rode my bike to the post office to deposit a couple of bills and some late Christmas letters. These are the Christmas letters to the people who wrote us, who we didn't initially write. Hope they don't take it the wrong way, seeing the late postmark on their letter.

Marisa is really showing now. All her old shirts and old pajama bottoms are stretched to their limits as they go around her. It's amazing. She's starting to wobble a little back and forth when she walks. She's been full of energy these three days. After all the research about the baby furniture, she found a great deal on a new four-piece set yesterday. It will be delivered when we can arrange a date.

There was a recovery guy in a meeting yesterday who told about selling his house while his wife was pregnant with their third child. "She was in full nesting mode, and I had the bright idea to sell the nest out from under us," he said. "I got sued trying to back out, but I wouldn't let her forget that she signed the paperwork to go along with it in the first place." He has a very upset wife right now, and it was a sobering reminder of how un-sober our actions can be, even after we quit drinking.

I feel guilty being sick, like I should be doing something, anything, to earn my keep. It's an old view that I have to earn my right to be here, to even exist. The Catholic faith I'm learning about doesn't come at things from the point of view that you have to earn everything. I'm hearing expressions like *heaven all the way to heaven*, and *the debt's already been paid on our behalf.* Father Rohr makes that statement about *heaven all the way to heaven.* He's saying that heaven isn't a giant SAT exam, where if we don't score well enough God won't open the doors. He's saying that Jesus came here to remind us to chill out and appreciate that this life is a gift, good and bad and however, it is a gift to be alive. "God doesn't love us because we are good. God loves us because God is good." It is good stuff, a gift to be receiving such Good News.

I had a 45 minute phone call with my dad today. He's really good at listening to me rattle through whatever I'm experiencing in life. I told him about reading my short stories with my family in New Jersey. He listens to me ramble and spoils me with his attention. I want to do that with our son, let the little guy know how special he is to me not just in words but through my actions. Listen to him connect his own dots as he goes about living his life.

I am grateful for recovery right now, for all the stories I have heard about people's victories and defeats. That's the joy and the pain of it. That's the preparation that will give me perspective to be able to listen to my son all the way through, from baby talk to teen-age talk to twenty-something and beyond.

In Catholic school, I'm learning about unconditional love. They have been saying that Jesus' main message is his example of unconditional love, that God loves us most when we deserve it the least. They say parenting is the closest example of unconditional love available to us, that we love our kids most when they deserve it the least.

In my family, we tested our dad, my brother and sister and I, as we turned into opinionated teenagers. My dad had an epiphany while he was in graduate school, and he vowed to never spank us again. We had probably gotten too big to spank anyway, but we didn't know that. We took Dad's vow and tested it. We weren't blatantly disrespectful, but close. We switched from being good preacher's kids to rebellious preacher's teenagers pretty dramatically. But now I wonder if what was really happening was that my dad was practicing unconditional love on us. Maybe dad was giving us space to grow up. Maybe he was loving us most when we deserved it least, as tiring, Texas teenagers.

When I think about how much it filled my soul to be able to speak with my dad 45 minutes earlier today, I also think about how much I cheated myself in earlier years. My dad had a four-way bypass heart surgery in September, 1991. That was 15 years ago this fall. That means I've had 15 extra years to catch up with my dad. How great is that? It's phenomenally great. Humberto's dad died in 1990 when Beto was only 20. How fortunate am I to be 37 with my dad still available?

My parents are good parents. They put their all into raising us three kids. They made sacrifices. They were good role models. They took parenting seriously. I know they said all those things parents are supposed to say, but it is amazing to me how much of it I ignored.

These last ten years, from 1996 to right now, I've done a lot of the growing up that should have happened when I was a kid, if I'd only been open to listening to my mom and dad. In 1996, I started doing the Landmark Education classes which would ultimately lead me to the cruise-ship class in the Mediterranean where I met Marisa. In those Landmark classes, I considered the possibility that maybe I shouldn't blame my parents for my troubles, how their job was to get me to 18 safely and after that, my life is what I make of it.

Those early Landmark classes were the first crack in my ego, and because of them, when my sister and mother led me to recovery, I was able to hear their love. Most people don't recover from alcohol or drugs until they've exhausted all the other options and made life very painful. In recovery meetings people say, *This was the last house on the block. Either it was recovery or institutions, jail, or death.*

To me, it seems that the Landmark classes made possible a shortcut—a bypass—of 10 or 15 years of pain. It is clear to me now that I can't drink, that my life is unmanageable left to my own devices in that area. It is clear to me now that I wouldn't be a husband, employee or future father if I still drank. But if I hadn't first done the Landmark courses, I don't think I could have surrendered to recovery; the intervention of my mom and sister would have failed. I still would have had to make a much bigger mess before realizing I had a problem. I would have gotten married, been an asshole, punished some poor woman who didn't deserve it, possibly punished our children, too, and I would have had one of those jump-off-the-bridge moments just like George Bailey in *It's a Wonderful Life*. That would have been me, and I would have either jumped, or, if I was lucky, I would have somehow gotten sober.

But that is not how it went. I bypassed that decade of despair and drama. That train wreck did not happen, and I am eternally grateful. Marisa is a centered, gracious, generous and beautiful woman. Watching her deal with the challenge of becoming pregnant, to see her receive the news from the specialist that we had less than a 2 percent chance of getting pregnant and not give up hope, and now to watch her take care of her body as it raises our unborn son—this is a gift from having chosen sobriety.

My parents told me how to be a good person. They showed me how to be a good person by their actions. But stubborn son that I am, I had to ignore all that and try to do life my way. My work in Landmark courses and my 12-Step work have given me a second chance to be the kind of person my parents worked so hard to raise. I'm grateful for that second chance.

Landmark and 12-Step work were both founded by men who messed up, but didn't give up. Werner Erhard, the founder of est and later Landmark, left his wife and children one day and moved to San Francisco. He had his epiphany on the Golden Gate Bridge and as a result made huge contributions to many millions of people. He later reconciled with his estranged family, a prodigal father returning, to receive their forgiveness and eventually contribute to their lives as well as so many others.[1] Bill Wilson, the founder of 12-Step work, was also a broken man, a dreamer whose family suffered as he went through the depths of disillusionment that alcohol wreaks on people who are allergic to it. His miracle came when he met another person with that same allergy, Dr. Bob, and together they created the 12 Steps and have healed many millions of people, too.[2]

When I hear the expression, "We stand on the shoulders of giants," I think of these two men and the spiritual debt that I owe them. Their lives were broken. They had lost everything, and yet from those ashes they arose and gave gifts to life that I then benefitted from many years later.

In Catholic school, they are telling us how Jesus didn't preach to the upper class rungs of society. People with enough time and money and power didn't listen to him. The only people who would hear his message were prostitutes and tax collectors, the bottom rungs. Father Rohr suggests that when we are at the bottom, when we have been broken by life and have cracks in our vessel, it is exactly through those cracks that the sunlight of the Spirit can enter. When we're on top, the Gospel is heard more mildly as in self-help. But when we are broken, then there is something really good in the Good News.

I am at the kitchen table on the afternoon of New Year's Eve. I'm married. I have a great job. My wife is pregnant after a fertility doctor told us it wasn't going to happen. I felt the baby's kick for the first time this week. My wife is full of joy and love. She's pregnant with a baby boy and with life. My parents had a wonderful conversation with me today. Does it get any better than this? Maybe it does, but I love this just the way it is.

[1] Bartley, William Warren. *Werner Erhard: The Transformation of a Man: The Founding of Est.* New York: Clarkson N. Potter, Ch. 4-6, 1978.

[2] *Alcoholics Anonymous: the Story of How Many Thousands of Men and Women Have Recovered from Alcoholism.* New York City: Alcoholics Anonymous World Services, Ch. 1, 2001.

Catholic Coaches — February 23, 2007

Dear Sister Catherine and the RICA (Rite of Christian Initiation in Adults) team:

Thank you for supporting our Catechumen community as we journey toward becoming part of the Catholic Church. My faith is growing as we walk this road together.

Life has prepared me to join the Catholic Church in several ways. I grew up in a practicing Christian family. My father is a duly ordained minister of Word and Sacrament in the Presbyterian Church, USA. My childhood was a direct gift from God, beautiful and blessed. My intention to become Catholic has everything to do with my desire to pay that gift forward in the family my wife Marisa and I are creating together.

My 20s were much less divine than my childhood. My will, not God's, was clearly running the show. My relationship to my faith became an intellectual practice. I told myself I could live off the interest from all those years sitting in church as a minister's son. I pursued all my worldly passions, some noble and some not. I earned a Master's Degree and went to work in Germany for three years. But I also drank too much and dated women with selfish intentions. That period of my life was a slow emptying of the vessel that God had so richly filled in my childhood.

God then granted me two epiphanies which opened me up to becoming Catholic. One was a transformational self-development seminar called the Landmark Forum that I took in 1996. The second was entering recovery in 2001. Together, these two shifts in my life took me away from my will, and opened me up to re-hearing God's Will for me and my life. Both of these experiences spotlighted my selfishness, my pride, and my fear. And they gave me tools to begin to re-connect with my Christian upbringing, and to live a life based in service versus fear.

When the student is ready, the teacher will appear. And that is exactly what happened shortly after my two epiphanies. The two teachers who appeared in my life are more like angels to me. The first teacher-angel is my wife Marisa, a life-long Catholic, my RCIA sponsor, and the richest blessing of my life. The second teacher-angel is Father Richard Rohr, a Franciscan Priest and Spiritual Director who has become my mentor and who has opened my heart to becoming Catholic. I've listened to hundreds of hours of his teachings on CDs in my car and heard him lecture twice, first at our own parish here of St. Monica's and second in Pasadena last year at a conference on politics and spirituality. He showed me that it was exactly the crack in my vessel—my alcoholism and fear and pride and self-centeredness—through which God enters into my life.

The most beautiful teaching of my Catholic journey thus far has been hearing Jesus' words when he preached the Sermon on the Mount, "Why do you worry over many things?" To me, that is the action and that is the promise of faith, to give up worrying over so many things. That is the Good News—we don't have to worry and live in fear and anxiety about things we can't control. God's presence is solid in my recovery program. And Jesus' words are certainly echoed by everything I learned in my transformational seminar—worry makes no difference and is a complete waste of time!

The Holy Spirit awoke in me through my two epiphanies. Now it is time to pick up my cross and be a stand for healing in the world, as Jesus asked us to do—to follow him, to forgive, and to heal.

While I will always try to arrange all the actors and scenery to how I think life should look, I will always fall short. My spiritual direction has taught me to turn my will and my life over to the care of a loving God and ask for His complete care and guidance. Becoming Catholic is the next step of that journey. It is a beginning, not an ending. It is an intimacy with my wife and a spiritual foundation for our beginning family.

Amen

Happy Birthday to Me — April 9, 2007

I am 38 years old today. It's Monday, and I'm sitting on a couch in our living room. I've been up 30 minutes. I changed my voicemail and e-mail to let work know that I am not coming in to the office today and Tuesday.

I woke up this morning from a vivid dream, full of sex and taxis late for the airport. After that, I couldn't go back to sleep. My wife is due in two weeks with our first child. I'm feeling anxious, and I'm surprised and disappointed that I am anxious. I think I was hoping it would be different, that our baby would give me new confidence. When we started our pregnancy journey many months ago, I started writing about it. That writing stopped around Christmas, and I've been in a different mode since then. Instead of letting my writing be an outlet for my creativity, I've been stressing and trying to work harder, so everything will turn out okay.

This promotion I got this year has not been turning out as I hoped. I don't know if I'm distracted with being an expectant daddy, or if the promotion was bigger than I am capable of, or if I am just impatient. I have never felt so out of control about work.

Marisa has planned a *babymoon* for us. Two days away from the office to celebrate both my 38th birthday and also our upcoming baby being born. But being out of the office makes me tense.

The writer Anne Lamott has a short story about how she has noticed that God gives her a distraction in area A in life, so that she will leave area B alone long enough for area B to be born. It's not just a metaphor; it is literally happening in our life. Our baby is about to be born.

I'm full of fear and dread about work, my area A. I'm organizing the house and making sure the bills are paid. Those are all distractions, pulling my attention away from the new event… that our baby is on the way, our area B.

Last week, I talked to my dad about this. I told him, "Dad, I've got a cold sore from the worrying. I'm not sure I'm dealing with all of this stress very well."

Dad laughed and said, "You come by it honestly. When you were born son, I broke out in hives. They gave me a gamma globulin shot just in case. By the day you arrived, I was hoarse and couldn't speak."

Thank you, Dad. How perfect was that to hear? My dad's father, my grandpa, died in 1977. That meant my father was only 33 when he lost his father. Here I am at 37 turning 38, five years more with my father than he had with his. I still have my father to go to for wisdom. What a gift.

Oh yeah. I became Catholic Saturday night at the Easter vigil at St. Monica's Church in Santa Monica. I would hate to call becoming Catholic a distraction, but even *that* got dramatic in this 11th hour. *Is this the right thing to do? Do I have all the information? Is there something I'm missing?* All these thoughts were racing through my head. It felt like joining the Corps of Cadets at Texas A&M all over again. *What's going to happen? How's it all going to play out?* Same questions.

My confirmation name is Paul. I've learned about Paul's influence on history by listening to Father Richard Rohr. Father Rohr asserts that Paul, probably more than the twelve apostles combined, was the greatest influence on Christianity becoming a religion. Paul was a mover and a shaker. Father Richard Rohr also says that Catholicism is an earthy, laughing, eating, drinking, family-making faith. *We absolutely insist on enjoying life,* we would say in recovery. He says that it's a celebratory, experiential religion, not a head-space, intellectual exercise. I want to find his book, <u>Why be Catholic?</u>[1], and reread that part, especially now that I have jumped in the boat of Catholicism.

Is writing my answer? Is this the way for me to tame the committee that convenes in my head with its never ending stream of observations, worries and concerns? To me, that is a life in need of creativity. Writing for me is that creativity, latent but budding and ready to blossom.

Happy Birthday to Me.

---

[1]Rohr, Richard, and Joseph Martos. *Why Be Catholic?: Understanding Our Experience and Tradition.* Cincinnati, OH: St. Anthony Messenger, 1989.

Two Days Past Due — April 23, 2007

Well here we are, two days past the due date. Our son won't be born on Aggie Muster. It's Monday morning and I've got a hint of a chest cold. My thinking is crap. It's not about all the blessings of my life. My head is full of imagined fears and problems. I don't want to go in to work. I'm concerned that I'll push too hard and make myself sick.

I want to make some big contribution, like Werner Erhard or Bill Wilson, founders of Landmark Education and 12-Step recovery, respectively. They are heroes to me, people who made huge contributions. My heroes have always been cowboys, or recovering alcoholics. How about Jesus, shunned by everyone and crucified naked outside the city walls? He was not an everyday hero. He came to heal, and people killed him for it.

I am wondering if being a parent is like being a hero. I don't know how to be either one, but for today, for starters, I'm writing. I'm noticing that my body is starting to relax. Marisa's calling me to breakfast from the other room. I'm joining the land of the living. I woke up at 7:40 and it is 8:18. It took 38 minutes today to feel like it was okay to participate in life. That's not too bad. Not too great and not too bad.

I'm ready for our little baby boy to arrive.

DADDY DIARIES ~

YEAR ONE

Happy Birth Night — Wednesday, April 25, 2007

It was 11:00 a.m. on Wednesday morning when Marisa finally went to sleep. Her leg twitched and she was out. Almost ten hours earlier, at 1:30 a.m., Marisa had safely delivered Paul Jackson Bonaventure Stafford, 8 pounds, 8 ounces and 21 inches long, via emergency C-section at UCLA Medical Center, Westwood. She was now asleep after 22 hours of labor that ended with major surgery.

She had five episodes of contractions during her labor, each one a series of waves building in intensity. The first episode started the day before, actually the middle of Tuesday night, at 2:15 a.m. We naively thought the baby would arrive by noon that day, but at 7:00 a.m., the contractions ended. There were more waves through the morning and afternoon, but each time, they tapered off. We spent a long day waiting.

The fifth and final wave of contractions started at 7:37 p.m. Sitting in our living room, we watched a Lakers basketball game on TV—they got beat up by Steve Nash and the Phoenix Suns, 126 – 98, to lose game two of the first round of the playoffs.

Not long after I turned off the game, the fifth episode of contractions strengthened and started to occur about five minutes apart. It was this fifth wave that brought us to the hospital. At about 10:30 p.m., having had contractions for three hours, Marisa started throwing up.

"It's time for you to call Dr. Kerr," she told me, her voice flat and direct. In between the throwing up and the contractions, I could tell it was time to go. I'd never seen her like this before, and I wanted to get to the hospital fast.

Dr. Mary Kerr, our amazing OBGYN, had been with us since our first baby doctor visit on October 27, 2006, a year and a half earlier. Now here we were, 41 weeks pregnant and ready to give birth. I called her, and she explained that the throwing up was normal, that Marisa had been riding the waves of the contractions all day long, and that it was normal for the up and down of the uterus to leave the woman feeling seasick.

"Come to the hospital. I'll see you there in a little while. Drive safely."

Marisa took a shower and then we put our bags in the car. I drove up Westwood Boulevard to UCLA, the same way I go to work so many days. Traffic was light, but I kept getting annoyed regardless. *What's with all the red lights?* I was thinking. Marisa did not feel well. She was doing the breathing exercises we had learned in class, sucking air in and forcing it out to stay focused. As we waited at a red light, I looked over at her. She was clearly hurting, and it was bothering me that I couldn't do anything about it. I was actually making it worse because her nausea worsened at every red light.

We arrived at the hospital about 11:45 p.m. There was no parking attendant on duty, so I parked in what I hoped was a legal parking spot. Marisa threw up again while I was trying to find a security guard. He helped us locate a wheelchair and I pushed Marisa down a long series of hallways inside the hospital to finally arrive at Labor and Delivery. We met Dr. Kerr and the doctor who administered the epidural. Dr. Kerr helped Marisa to the restroom and then put some pressure on the lower part of her back to help relieve the pain. It was about 1:00 a.m., and everything was looking good. Dr. Kerr insisted that we both get some sleep, hinting that there was plenty of action still to come and we should be rested for it.

Marisa was secured in her hospital bed with all the monitors hooked up and attached. Her room had a little sofa off to the side which Dr. Kerr, much to my surprise, made up with sheets, blankets and a pillow so I could rest and be in the same room with Marisa. The lights were lowered. Dr. Kerr stepped away. I took off my shoes and put them under the sofa. The nurse asked Marisa to roll over on her other side to check something in the fetal monitor, then left. It was quiet and dark.

"I love you honey," I said.

"I love you, too." Marisa sounded exhausted and far away.

I felt safe for the first time all day. We were here at the UCLA hospital. The doctors were nearby. There were nurses and monitors and lights, and Marisa was in a hospital bed. This was good. We would sleep a few hours, I figured, and in the morning Marisa would deliver the baby.

Then all heck broke loose.

The nurse came back, checking the monitor and abruptly summoning Dr. Kerr. Instantly, several observant, dressed-like-doctor people appeared at Marisa's bedside. The soft lights were obliterated as full room lighting was turned on. Marisa looked over at me, a confused expression on her face, and I watched as people started unhooking the monitors and sitting her up in bed.

"We're going to take you across the hallway, Marisa," one of the white coats said. "It's an operating room. It doesn't mean we are going to operate, but we want to get a better look at the baby."

Dr. Kerr explained and coordinated the activities. In an instant, *whoosh*, Marisa's bed turned into a moving vehicle and she was wheeled away.

"Daddy, you're going to need to put on these scrubs, so you can come over, too." A large nurse was smiling at me and showing me how to pull on the surgical overcoat, hairnet, booties and facemask. "It's okay, honey," she said noticing my awkwardness. "There's plenty of time."

How are my shoes going to fit in these little booties? Wasn't I wearing these shoes doing yard work last weekend? That can't be too sanitary. My thoughts were erratic, but within minutes I was across the hall in the operating room, where a flurry of doctors and nurses were fully engaged in some very urgent tasks.

The lights were bright, and from my position I could see the backs of the doctors, shoulder to shoulder, over Marisa's belly. (Marisa, with her characteristic good humor, would later say, "It was like a NASCAR pit stop in there!") Someone guided me to a seat by Marisa's head. I couldn't see the surgery, only the back of a curtain that had been thrown up to close off the theater of operations from our view. But I could hold Marisa's hand and look at her. Her hair was tucked away underneath a surgery cap. I couldn't tell from her expression how she was doing.

"You guys are doing great," Dr. Kerr said from behind the curtain that I now realized separated us from the C-Section that was proceeding. "The baby's heart rate dropped, and after all that time, it's time for this little guy to be born. Daddy, you be with Mommy. Mommy, you're doing great."

I sat on my little stool and held Marisa's hand. I was terrified. I had no control over what was going on. If something went wrong, there was nothing I could do. Surgery was never talked about in all those classes we went to on childbirth education. We had no preparation for this, the bright lights and a curtain, lots of doctors and scary sounds. The only familiar thing was Dr. Kerr's voice, which I clung to for comfort. She was clearly directing the operation, and every now and again, she'd aim some warm words at us through the curtain.

"You're doing great, sweetie, and we're doing fine over here," Dr. Kerr shared some solace while she kept the operation moving.

"I love you, love. You're doing great," I said and looked down at Marisa.

"I'm cold," she replied. There was nothing I could do about that, and so I sat there silently with her hand in mine.

Then there was a cry, a big, beautiful cry. It filled the room and it filled my heart, our baby coming into the world.

"Oh, we've got a big baby boy here, Mommy!" Dr. Kerr told us from behind the curtain. "Daddy, you need to come around here and see your son."

I stood up like a robot, following the doctor's instructions.

"Who is the redhead in the family?" asked a nurse, while someone else led me over to the warming table where our little son had been placed and was quickly surrounded by many hands.

"Do you want to cut the cord, Daddy?"

"Huh? Sure. Okay," I replied, and my hands closed on the scissors—

Snip!

One, two, three, *boom*. It was all going so fast. The many doctors around our son were wiping and cleaning and checking and swabbing, and before it seemed possible, they had wrapped him up in a soft blanket and placed him into my arms.

"Now Poppa, you take your son back to Mommy while we finish up here." Dr. Kerr motioned me back to my stool behind the curtain. She was completely mindful of the two very different worlds happening at once—her surgery on Marisa and us holding our first child.

I held our tiny papoose in front of Marisa. She started crying. "He's so beautiful. He's so beautiful." Her eyes ran all over our new little baby. I stared, too. There was so much going on in the room but we were in our own little bubble. He looked like a baby Buddha, calm and curious and peaceful. His eyelids slowly blinked open and closed, as he took everything around him in.

In our Lamaze class, we were asked to hold our spouse's hand and then take the hand of another person who we didn't know as well. This was to demonstrate what it's like to pick up your own child vs. someone else's child. Now, I fully understood that experience. I was handed tiny Paul Jackson and went to sit next to Marisa. Holding him was the most natural thing, and at the same time, like nothing I'd ever experienced.

I don't remember the rest of the surgery, it's all a blur. Sometime later we were all three in a recovery room, baby safe in Mommy's arms, Mommy's belly safely sewn back together. There was another woman in the room who was still in labor. I had forgotten to bring the camera bag in from the car, so I left for a few minutes to get it. I had also forgotten the special box at home in which we intended to collect any umbilical cord blood for possible stem cell use later, but we wouldn't even realize this for while. We took pictures and made wake-up calls to all the new grandparents—Marisa let me call my parents first—then to my sister Lisa, to Marisa's sister Bonnie and several friends. We said the height and weight, that it was a C-section, that everyone was okay. There was love on the line. I took a picture of baby Jack with my camera phone and e-mailed it out. That photo would be the screensaver on my phone for the next two years.

I stepped away later and bought a Sprite from a vending machine down the hall. I was still in the new-baby section, so it must have been easy for anyone to tell.

"You just have a baby?" a stranger asked me. "Congratulations."

I was still stunned; amazed that it was all really happening.

A nurse came in, and together we gave Jack a sponge bath. He looked so perfect. His skin was so soft. His legs looked so long. I helped the nurse but mostly stared and smiled. His hair was blond, with strawberry highlights. He opened his eyes every now and then, but they didn't seem to focus, just stared straight ahead, looking into space.

I officially changed two diapers that night, two more than I had changed my entire life prior. Marisa nursed him three times, with the help of Dr. Kerr who came in and helped Marisa establish the *latch*.

"Hold your breast like a hamburger and place it under his nose," she explained. "He'll know what to do next. He should be a hungry guy after what he's been through. Your colostrum will flow for a day or two before your milk comes in, but that ought to do him for now."

It was 11:00 a.m. on this morning after the night he was born, and Marisa finally closed her eyes and fell asleep. *Yeah!*

I looked over to see the little guy wrapped up like a baby burrito in his plastic see-through isolator crib at the foot of Marisa's hospital bed. He had his little stocking cap on and was swaddled in a white cotton blanket, angled up, so his head was slightly above his feet. Mommy was finally asleep. I took a few minutes to write and capture some notes of memories. Nobody came into the room, and I, too, fell into a deep and much needed sleep.

Day One — April 25, 2007

Day One, still Wednesday, began a few short hours later when baby Jack—a name we decided to call Paul Jackson Bonaventure Stafford some time later—woke up hungry. Marisa would be a very light sleeper for most of the hospital stay—except for that deep but short nap from 11 a.m. to 2 p.m.—and most of the next two years. Even in the hospital with all the professional care so close, she would sleep lightly and wake up at the smallest sound from Jack. Sometimes he would make small noises, gentle coos and chirps, but other times he would let out screams that amazed me with their power. Then, after a meal or after a poop, he'd calm down quickly and be back to a quiet coo.

Jack, we would learn, slept for only short periods of time. We'd been warned that our newborn's sleeping patterns would be strange, and they were. It didn't help that Jack was born in the middle of the night, throwing off our days and nights from any semblance of normal circadian rhythms.

Dr. Kerr came and checked on Marisa's C-Section. The incision was a low, horizontal line on the front of her tummy, covered with special medical tape that would remain in place for the next two weeks. Marisa was feeling exhausted but relieved that Dr. Kerr had come, and even though she was groggy from the pain medication, she was intent on feeding Jack successfully. Dr. Kerr inquired about how Marisa was doing with the breastfeeding and asked if we had any questions. Marisa downloaded a long list, and Dr. Kerr responded to all, large and small. I sat and listened, seeing Marisa's relief as she got helpful advice from a competent source.

Dr. Kerr was our guide person for everything, from dealing with HR departments and hospitals and visitors, to breastfeeding and sleeping and eating. It seemed like there was so much to know and we didn't know anything. She made sure Marisa did not skimp on her pain medicine given to her for her C-section. She said pain was like a hole, and it was best to not fall in too deep. This was good advice, as Marisa has a habit of powering through pain, instead of taking medicine for relief.

Dr. Kerr's *how tos* were distinct from all the other advice the world was giving us. It was the quality, the timing, the empathy and the accountability—that combination—that made her input so useful, so nourishing and compassionate. I wondered how I could possibly acknowledge our appreciation of her for all her advice and perspective. It was like saying thank you to God.

I'm sure doctors have a name for the feeling of hero worship I had for Dr. Kerr—doctors have a name for everything. Whatever it's called, it was brilliant to experience. I couldn't think of the last time somebody so impressed me, so exceeded my expectations on something so important.

Our days stayed mixed up. The first night, Jack was awake from midnight to about 6:00 a.m. We would feed him, and he would be satisfied for a little while, then he would start crying again, and we would do a repeat. He was a hungry little guy, hungry a lot. At one point, after he finished eating, I held him in my arms and watched him calm down. I could feel him soft and warm all over. His tiny knees touched my hand as I held him, and I stroked his soft, tender head. I was getting better at swaddling him. The right snugness of swaddle helped settle him down, and my wraps were improving with practice.

And there were phone calls. Marisa's Uncle Jeff called that first evening and wanted to know, "Have you asked little Jack why he picked you to be his parents yet?" It was a cool question. It made me think about heaven and again about the opening scene in the movie *It's a Wonderful Life*, when the angels are talking about what was going on down below. What if Jack had been an angel and really did pick us, from all the parents in the world waiting to have a child? I noticed that people would say brilliant and fascinating things like this around the baby—how he brought out the beautiful side of people. I loved Uncle Jeff's question, and reflected that he was the one who introduced Marisa to Landmark classes which ultimately meant we met on our cruise.

Speaking with my sister Lisa, I was surprised at how many questions she asked about the whole process. I always assume my sister knows everything, because she is such a curious person, but this was new for her, too, and she was learning along with us.

With our digital camera, a phone camera, an old fashioned film camera and a video recorder, we took tons of pictures during our stay in the hospital. We snapped and filmed and I joked that we were recording every six seconds of Jack's life so far.

Marisa was joy-filled. She was on another channel, in another realm altogether. Dr. Kerr kept reminding her to take her pain medication and to *sleep when the baby sleeps*. She did this, but she was on a baby high that must have way surpassed the power of the medicine. She was completely joyous. She kept asking questions every time someone entered our room. No one got to leave until they gave us at least one more tip for taking care of our Jack. We were in our little cocoon inside our hospital room, and we felt protected and safe, eager to soak up the gifts of wisdom and contribution from all who entered.

Hospital Days — April 26 - 28, 2007

Day Two

By Day Two, the lack of sleep was starting to catch up for both of us. The only time Jack slept that first night of Day One was when he was lying on his mom's tummy or cradled next to her in the hook of her arm. He no longer wanted any part of that plastic bassinette at the foot of her hospital bed. This kept us both wakeful and our sleep sporadic. We were still turned around, days and nights blending together, and the tiredness was rapidly replacing our initial euphoria.

Because UCLA is a teaching hospital, a parade of young doctors passed through our room day and night, starting with our very first morning. The quantity of doctors should have been reassuring, but most of them were so young—by young I mean younger than us—that I couldn't get the words *Doogie Howser* out of my head. They were polite and smart, but their bedside manner seemed stiff, almost textbook, as if lifted from page 53 of the new Doctor's Manual: *Walk into the patient's room with confidence. Be nice. Be friendly.*

At 6:00 a.m. on Day Two, the parade began and continued for about a half hour. "Is there anything else I can answer for you, Mrs. Stafford?" finally asked one of the doctors who was very thin, very Indian, very polite—and very young.

Exhausted, Marisa raised her arm slowly, as if to point at the twelve-year old doctor, and replied, "Yes..." She took a deep breath before continuing. "I want you... to tell us... how to get him... to sleep in there." She moved her finger to point at the bassinette at the foot of her bed, the crib that Jack had decided during the night was no longer good enough to sleep in.

Marisa waited for an answer. "...Well, um, he should...um...." came the impish reply, and very quietly our Indian Doogie Howser and all his friends from band camp backed out of the room to go find easier tasks, like brain surgery.

Around 7:00 a.m., Jack did go to sleep in his bassinette, and by 9:00 a.m., mercifully, his mommy was asleep, too. It appeared that how it was going to work was that when baby finally ate enough and fell asleep, Mom would cry briefly—I think just from relief he was finally sleeping and exhaustion in general—and nap lightly for 15 minutes, wake up, call loved ones to verify that all this was normal, order some breakfast, nap for 10 minutes, wake up when the nurses came, eat breakfast, make a few more calls. Only after all that, nearly two hours of activity, would Marisa be reassured enough to go to sleep for real for herself, another deep, leg-muscles-kicking sleep. The kind of sleep I knew she needed.

I slipped out into the hallway and made a couple of quiet calls myself. Every time I talked to my dad, my mom, my sister and brother, I could hear the joy in their voices. The joy that came from family and friends over this birth was contagious and overflowing. It gave me energy. Jack made my own heart skip, seeing him move or turn or stretch. It caught me off guard each time.

I was already working on nicknames. He was a little... potato, burrito, frog, prince, angel, cutie, pumpkin... I was loving his different noises, cooing, crying, even the screaming when he let go and emptied his lungs, the God-that's-gotta-hurt kind of screaming.

The main (and only) smile we saw on his face was when the lactation consultant tickled his feet. That smile was really distinct, and since she made it happen so easily, we thought we'd see him smile a lot, but that was the only time. She was the mother of six kids, five she had in her 20s and a bonus baby she had when she was 39 who she nursed up to age four.

She gave us all kinds of tips. She showed how to stick a finger in the side of Jack's mouth and break the seal when he'd latched on to the breast but was no longer sucking and had fallen asleep. How to pick him up with a blanket, or by putting one hand under his head and the other under his butt. She told us to get two *boppy* pillows for back home to help prevent back strain when Marisa nursed him sitting up. Ear, shoulder, hip—Line those up to get the baby in position to nurse. She told us about Lanolin, a miracle cream that did the trick for sore nipples.

She showed Marisa how to side nurse, laughing as she said, "Side nursing is not academy approved, because they worry a mom could fall asleep and roll over onto the baby. But human beings have been doing it for thousands of years, so it's something you should know about." She gave us her phone number. I don't think we ever called her, but it was nice to have.

Visitors started to come by for the first time on Thursday, officially Day Two in the hospital.

My sponsor in recovery, Everett, came in the afternoon to meet Paul Jackson. Everett was the first non-hospital person to see Jack. "He is a little slice of God," said Everett as he cradled Jack. This was a special moment. Everett had been my sponsor ever since we had moved to Los Angeles, five years earlier. He was an extra father to me and had coached me through my engagement, my wedding, our first married years, my challenges at work, and our other pregnancy. He was at the Easter Vigil three weeks earlier when I had become a Catholic. Here he was holding Jack and smiling at Marisa and putting words to the feelings that were all over me. Yes, I thought, Jack is a little slice of God. This whole experience is.

Deb and Vickie from work came by with a giant balloon and hugs and smiles. My office was on the other side of campus, but it seemed like another planet. A few hours later, our other friends, Herb and Corbel, came to see Jack. Corbel seemed even less knowledgeable than me about babies, and I noticed myself starting to feel like an expert by comparison. How far I had come in just two days!

Day Two's night sleeping was still mostly interrupted, but better. Marisa wore her abdominal binder and took her medicine. Jack beat to his own drummer. He was starting to use the isolator in the day time, but at night, he only wanted mommy. We were learning to make Mommy sleep when Jack slept.

Day Three

The biggest interruption on the morning of Friday, Day Three was not the doctor parade, but the grey-haired juice-nurse. Was she a volunteer? Was she slightly loopy? It was hard to tell, but she was definitely on the deaf side. Jack was still asleep when she came in, and before we could whisper loud enough for her to hear, she was throwing open the curtains with full fanfare, as if showing us some million dollar prize outside in the hospital parking lot. We were tired and cranky, and Jack woke up with the noise and light. But after she left, we had to laugh. Our juice-nurse had a great, Irish accent and she meant well, but she was so very *deaf*.

Jack's weight was down 4.5% by Friday morning. We were told that was normal. Weight would double by four months, triple by one year, and quadruple at two years, they said. He was a big kid to begin with, so we would see. The doctors checked him for jaundice along with all sorts of other things. He looked healthy to me, and I was grateful for that.

Day Three was a big day, as Grandma Barbara Szem, Marisa's mom, would arrive in the afternoon. She was flying in from South Carolina. Barbara is the mother of five children and now grandmother to nine, and I couldn't wait for her to arrive. She is the closest of the two redheads in the family to Jack (my grandmother Bobby Dear is the other contributor to Jack's hair color).

In my mind, Barbara would quell any lingering anxiety Marisa had about doing the right thing and tell us everything we wanted to know that all our Doogies didn't learn in medical school. Barbara coming was like Julia Childs swinging by to lend a hand right before you were hosting a big dinner party. The cavalry was coming.

I picked Barbara up at LAX airport Friday afternoon. It was my first time leaving the hospital since we had checked in for our midnight delivery, some 60 hours and a life time earlier. It was a strange feeling to be back in the world again. I'd gotten into hospital interior mode, and the California sunshine seemed especially bright. I hoped the world hadn't changed too much in the three days, and found myself wanting to slow people down for a minute, to tell them how miraculous things really are.

A new baby is born. His Grandmother is here. This is big, great news!

Barbara and I found each other by cell phone and I picked her up curbside. "I'm wearing a green hat," she had told me.

"How are you?"

"Great."

"Your flight?"

"Very nice." Big smiles, like we were kids sharing the best possible secret. Hugs. Luggage. Into the car and away.

"I'll take the surface streets to stay off the Friday freeway. We can swing by the house or we can go straight to the hospital. Which do you prefer?"

"Hospital, please. How long is the ride?" she asked, staring ahead and smiling. She wanted to be one place and one place only.

Sepulveda snaked its way up west Los Angeles as we drove along and made small talk. Even though I knew the drive from countless mornings commuting, I still felt like a kid in a station wagon who can't wait to get to Six Flags. I couldn't wait to get Barbara to her daughter and new grandson. I wanted them to see each other. I knew how much it would mean to Marisa, and I was learning as we drove how much it meant to Barbara. I had never seen my mother-in-law so excited.

Barbara is a petite woman who was once a court stenographer. Now she is the office manager for an architectural firm building high-end homes in South Carolina. What I love about my mother-in-law is her perspective and her way with people. She watches and observes. She asks and listens. She is one of the anchors of my wife's life and now mine, too. She gave Marisa an embroidered pillow with the words, *Always my daughter, Now too my friend.* That captures it.

Soon we arrived, and I was glad to be back in the dim cocoon of our hospital room. Baby Jack met his grandma for the first time. Cameras clicked. He was wrapped up burrito-like in his swaddle. Grandma held him and smiled, and then held him and smiled some more. She has eight other wonderful grandchildren, but it had been over ten years since any of them had been as new and small as Jack.

Our giant, three foot tall *It's a Boy* balloon from Deb and Vickie stood guard over us. I continued to take too many pictures with all the devices we had, including low resolution cell phone pictures to forward to my mom and dad.

Our last visit on Day Three was from Kathy, my other colleague who is the mother of three young kids. She *oohed* and *aahed* about how tiny new babies are. Kathy would move her family to northern California a year later and in the process, donate a four-box library of children's books to us, many of which became Jack's favorites.

I drove Grandma Szem to our home and then returned to the hospital. That night's sleep was the best yet, but it was still only in two hour blocks. Diapers and nursing and diapers and nursing. Marisa was doing better than me. I was trying to keep up, but it was weird and disorienting. "Don't forget, sleep deprivation is a form of torture," Dr. Kerr told us on one visit. She said it so sweetly, but *torture* was exactly what it felt like having so much sleep taken away from me.

Day Four

Saturday morning, Dr. Kerr came one more time for the circumcision. She asked if Marisa and/or I wanted to accompany Jack. Marisa deferred, so I went with her. We placed Jack in a little mobile baby cart and twisted down several corridors to a procedure room.

I had thought about circumcision during the pregnancy. It didn't make sense to me, the more I learned about it. It seemed that there was no longer any scientific consensus, and that the older ideas of why circumcision might be good had all been discredited. The best answers I got were vague ones—*so he'll look like daddy*. This seemed hardly enough to merit cutting my son.

I had a guilty, slightly sick feeling as I watched Dr. Kerr take out her tools and begin to operate on Jack. It was one moment, a brief little set of seconds and minutes, but on the other side of that moment, life would be forever different. I took a breath and wondered if lots of parent moments were going to be like this. I wondered how many moments like this would transpire for Jack. I wondered how many of those moments I would get right as a parent, and how many I would regret. Jack cried out briefly, but it was over very fast, and we took him back to Mommy with his bandage. He was fine.

It was our last day in the hospital, early Saturday evening just before dark, when we drove home with our new baby. There were four of us in the car, including Grandma Szem. It was the first time to use our new baby car seat. Marisa was in the back with Jack. We were all tired. It was disorienting to leave the safety of the nurses and doctors. We were entrusted with the care and feeding of our little new person, which seemed like a huge, overwhelming responsibility had abruptly landed on our shoulders.

Having grandma with us was a blessing. She didn't give orders or instructions. She and Marisa have such a loving, respectful relationship that much of their communication seemed to be in the things unsaid. She had a way of smoothing things and helping us land back into our completely new life with our first baby.

Dr. Kerr had helped bring Jack into the world. Grandma Szem now helped bring us into the world with Jack.

Thank You, Doctor Mary Kerr — April 30, 2007

Thank you Doctor Mary Kerr,

You were our OBGYN for the successful birth of our first child, Paul Jackson Bonaventure Stafford. He was born April 25, 2007 at 1:30 in the morning.

You weren't home with your own husband and three sons the night our son came into the world. You were with us, and we want to say thank you to you for that.

We want to thank you for all the things you did that we know about – all of the office visits where you answered questions and talked us through doubts and gave us perspective and hope and nourishment during our pregnancy. Those were things we saw and experienced ourselves. Thank you for all of that.

We also want to thank you for all those things you did that we will never know about. All the things you did along the way that culminated in you taking my wife across the hallway and conducting a C-section delivery of our son and a successful operation to put Marisa back together.

Thank you for deciding to be a doctor. I don't know if you have doctors in your family or if you are the first one. Either way, somewhere back in high school or college you decided to do this. I want to thank you for making that decision.

Thanks for sticking with it – biology and chemistry and physiology and internships and residencies, and all of it. I'm sure there are easier things to study. Thank you for all those times you studied a little bit harder. Thank you for getting out of bed all those mornings to go and face those exams. Thank you for the lack of sleep you must have endured. Thank you for the tradeoffs you made of leisure and friends and family. Those tradeoffs that started way before our midnight rendezvous with you the night of our son's delivery. Thank you for all of that.

We have many loving nicknames for you: Mary K, Doctor K, MKDK, and my own favorite, Glenda the Good Witch from the *Wizard of Oz*, referring to your fantastic positive outlook.

Your bedside manner is at the edge of the bell curve. What the Four Seasons is to a vacation, you are to a bedside visit. We would come home after a session with you and replay everything we could remember of your coaching and perspective. We'd comment on your use of language and your ability to articulate your ideas in ways that factored for dealing with patients of all different backgrounds and points of view.

Sweetie, Honey, You Guys. You had all your little nicknames for us each time you swept into the exam room to see us. You always made the little happy face as you applied the ultrasound jelly to Marisa's tummy. On the ultrasound printouts, you always penned in the body part that had been photographed and labeled it so that we would know later what we were looking at. You didn't have to do that, but you did it every single time.

You told us this little guy was lucky to have us for parents. You said that having a little boy would be wonderful, that little boys are a joy to raise, and that they only have two speeds, on and off. (We knew, however, that if we'd had a girl, you would have also shared something miraculous about little girls, too.)

And that night, after a day of on-again-off-again contractions, when we called you, and you said you would meet us at the hospital, you were our angel. You met us. You examined Marisa. You saw she was exhausted from a day of contractions and only 20 minutes of sleep. You pushed on her back to relieve the pain as the contractions came. You took her into the bathroom to help her when that was needed.

You told her the epidural would be fine and made sure our anesthesiologist was ready to get us set up correctly. And when you said that we should get some sleep that night, you actually put sheets on the couch for me, the floating father, to be in the room with my soon-to-give-birth wife. Doctors don't put sheets on couches. Or so I thought, before I met you.

Then, only 20 minutes later, our little baby showed signs of distress on the monitor. You said, "Sweetie, I want to ask you to roll on one side. Okay, now the other. Okay, now I'm going to tickle the baby's head. Okay. Sweetie, we are going to take you across the hall to a different room. It's an operating room. It doesn't mean necessarily that we are going to operate, but we think we can get a better picture of how the baby's doing there."

All said in your delicate and sensitive voice, good Glenda spreading magic dust. As I sat at the head of the operating table, behind the curtain so I could be near Marisa, I heard the other voice you have, the field general directing the troops. You were in charge of Marisa's delivery and operation. There was no doubt about that.

It was exactly what we wanted to hear, the voice of competence, purpose and direction. We knew that you were going to make sure everything came out alright.

"Do you want to come see your son, Poppa?" I heard someone say, and looked to see one of the nurses holding Paul Jackson in her hands. More questions followed—"Who's the redhead in the family? Do you want to cut the umbilical cord, Dad?"—while you kept operating on Marisa.

When it was all over, and I thanked you in person, you said that your work was a joy, that you got to share very special moments with people. "These moments make the highlight reel," you said, using a movie metaphor to acknowledge what was definitely one of the greatest moments of my life.

From behind the curtain, I heard Paul Jackson let out his first cry as you lifted him out of Marisa. I peeked over and saw his glistening body, so tiny and red. I walked over to the warming table where the three other attendants had taken him and were working on him. I glanced to my right and saw enough to know my wife's body was open on the operating table, her life in the balance.

In that moment, I was torn between two totally distinct worlds. There was our new son and the joy of welcoming him into the world. And there was my wife lying helpless on the operating table, her life now in your hands. As I glanced from our baby to Marisa, it struck me that I am uninterested in living my life without this woman. Both of these in parallel—so huge, so enormous to me—my whole life in this operating room. And you were successfully running the show to its conclusion, fully in control of all of it.

All in a day's work for you. All in a lifetime's memory for me.

Thank you Doctor Mary Kerr. Thank you for being *the One* to do it all. Thank you for making it look so easy. Thank you for your excellence. Thank you for your love. Marisa and I are very clear that you are an angel.

With love and appreciation,

Marisa Szem-Stafford and Dylan Stafford,

Happy parents of Paul Jackson Bonaventure Stafford

Evening Prayers — April 30, 2007

Paul Jackson Bonaventure Stafford, Marisa Lynn Szem-Stafford, and Barbara Szem are all three asleep in the house. The voice of Father Richard Rohr is quietly coming through the CD player in Paul Jackson Bonaventure's room, delivering a lecture on the subject of masculine spirituality. It's heavenly white noise for my sleeping son, and I can't help but think it's good for him to listen to a future saint, since he's named for two of them—*Paul* and *Bonaventure*.

Today I held him on my chest as I sat in the rocking chair watching the basketball game in the living room. He likes to curl on his side, scrunching up in his swaddling blanket and dozing off. If he starts to fuss, I can pat his back or murmur deeply or rock the chair, and he seems to calm back into his quiet sleep.

This being the fifth day since his birth, Marisa had a more normal day than previously. After breakfast, she got some good sleep from about 10:30-1:00 p.m. Paul Jackson is eating very well. We're happy with the throughput into his diapers, indicating his digestion has kicked in and everything is working as it should.

Marisa has a rash, so I went to the 24 hour pharmacy up at the Ralph's grocery store across the street from our UCLA Medical Center to pick up her prescription. Dr. Mary Kerr continues as our OBGYN, and tomorrow we see a new doctor, our pediatrician. New faces and new places. We're sad that Dr. Kerr can't be our pediatrician, too.

"Too hard," she told us when we asked her why. "Babies with colds take a lot of work." I smiled inside thinking her job as an OBGYN was no cake walk.

At the moment, I'm peaceful about this whole thing. Thank you God for that peace. There's not a lot to do but *be here now*. That is enough. What will I do with the rest of this life? Hopefully the peaceful feeling will continue.

Marisa is the best wife in the world. She's arranged every element of her life to make room for a healthy, happy pregnancy and birth, the miracle of Paul Jackson. Mentally, physically, psychologically, intellectually, ontologically, family-wise, work-wise, friend-wise. She changed her entire way of living to make room for Paul Jackson. He must have liked what he saw her doing in getting ready to be his mom, and he chose us, as Uncle Jeff suggested, for his parents. We're blessed by that.

Thank you God, for connecting me to life. Recovery connected me to being a player among players. Catholicism connected me to the tradition of faith and the saints and the history of mystics of over 2000 years. Now parenthood and fatherhood connects me to the hopes and wishes and possibilities of fathers from the beginning of time. It connects me to the fears and worries, too—the other half of the coin.

Listening more to Father Rohr's CD on masculine spirituality, I'm learning how all societies throughout history have known that the uninitiated male not bonded to the community was not a good thing. Uninitiated boys grow up to be lonely, bitter, and disconnected men. Thank you God, for sparing me that outcome in life. Recovery has been an important initiation in my life, and I thank you for my powerlessness over alcohol. Thank you that my life is unmanageable, and that You, a power greater than myself whom I choose to call God, daily restores me to sanity and blesses my life. Thank you for that peace. Power, freedom and peace of mind. All of these and more I'm learning are part of the journey I'm on.

I made a tongue-clicking noise to soothe a squirming Paul Jackson. Where did that particular response come from? I could have heard it from another parent, or it could be instinctual, which is what I prefer to believe. Jack responded to it and he settled.

He calms in my presence. I've bonded with him already. They said at the hospital that you cannot have too much physical contact with your infant the first two months, as he's used to being held 24/7 in the womb. I worked on that today with him, and in fact, choose to see that I've been working on that all year, watching lots of basketball on TV to prepare me for lots of rocking chair time with my new son. I've never watched as much basketball as I have this year.

My new son. It's decadent to say that. It's so rich. It's distinct from when I say *our new son*, which I've said mostly. *My new son* is almost too much.

Sitting around the kitchen table today, we all three looked at my baby album photos. How closely Paul Jackson looks like the photos of me as a baby. The slope of our eyes, our noses and ears. The length and even the hue of our hair. Cheeks and lips. I want to put two similarly posed snapshots side by side. It's a deliciously decadent experience, seeing myself in my child.

Grandma Barbara is a peaceful, wonderful guest. She has seen so much in her life with her own five children and now nine grandchildren. She is gentle and magnificent with supporting us. She loves her newest grandson and dotes on him from an easy distance.

My mother will come later this week. She'll be seeing her very first grandchild for the first time. How magnificent will that be, her first view of Paul Jackson? That will be off-the-scale, amazingly fantastic.

I saw a magazine with a made-up list of the ten things to do before you die. I clipped it out, because I liked the idea. Now I'm realizing that it didn't have anything about creating a life partner or being a parent. Shame. They missed two big ones.

Lutz once told me the Germans say that every man needs to do three things: Build a house, plant a tree, have a son. I love the simplicity of that saying. More so, I love the perspective that life has to offer me now at age 38, experiencing fertility, pregnancy and birth with my wife Marisa. We have a home, and I've planted lots of trees, both in California and in Texas. Now we have a child, and that makes for one overflowing basket of love and life.

I'm thinking about teachings I've learned in sobriety and in becoming a Catholic. *Practice being undeserving,* that is one lesson I've been taught. God's grace is unearned and undeserved. It is pure gift; the *divine indwelling* Father Rohr calls it, unearned in me, unearned in everyone. *Practice gratitude,* which is another key lesson. We all want to be known as people who can contribute something. What does it take for us to be known as people who can receive with equal grace? There is nowhere to be but right here, right now.

I feel the sleepies coming over me. There is a deep peace coming from the table where my elbows are resting. There is a peace in the muscles of my neck. There is peace in the warmth of my sweatshirt. There is peace in my sobriety. There is peace in my love of my family. There is peace in the possibility of the future. There is peace with my past, not wishing to shut the door on it, but seeing how it could be useful to others.

Thank you God, for the strength for the journey. Thank you for the wisdom and balance and perspective. Thank you for Paul Jackson Bonaventure Stafford and my relationship with Marisa, his mom.

Grandma "G" — May 3, 2007

Today I picked up Grandma Ginny, or Grandma G as my mother has decided she wants to be called, and brought her to her first-ever grandchild. Both my mom's sisters have been grandmothers for a while. She's waited patiently and today her patience was rewarded.

What I love about my mom is that she's fierce even though she rarely shows it. She's steady steel behind a beautiful smile and a downward, soft glance. I call her a tiger mom, and she hates it when I talk like this about her. But that is what she represents to me, the background strength that always held our family together.

Mom taught me about dealing with people. Dad taught me about dealing with life, but Mom showed me about dealing with all those people you meet, running through the hallways of life. Mom was the homecoming queen of her high school in Tempe, Arizona, and her sorority president at Trinity University in San Antonio. She chose the tall preacher-man to be her life's partner. How'd she make that choice? She liked that he had played violin in the orchestra. She liked that he had been a basketball player. She liked his passion and that love of life he has, and she liked his humor.

They raised us three kids in the 21,000 person hamlet of Denison. It wasn't even a suburb, rather a stand-alone, small town on the border with Oklahoma. Denison was a destination for all the kids in the surrounding, "really small" small towns like Bells and Pottsboro and Whitewright. Their kids came to our main street on Saturday nights to drive up and down the drag. Sometimes we made a Saturday evening run to Safeway with Mom. Seeing the teens in their cars was beyond exotic, it was intoxicating, as I'm sure a lot of them were.

How did Mom adjust to this small town living? I think it was great when we were kids. I think it was great, but did she? My mom is adventurous. She is the one who backpacked Europe with her girlfriend during college then took my dad to Europe in 1967 after they got married.

She tells me that when she took my dad to Oslo, Norway, to the outdoor Vigeland sculpture garden, that it was a test. If Dad liked the garden, then they were going to work out as a couple. If he didn't… well that might be bad news. It turned out that he loved the garden. He took rolls of film and logged it all in his diary. He passed her test with flying colors and he didn't even know there was an exam happening.

Marisa, her mom and Jackson stayed behind at the house while I drove to LAX to retrieve my mom from her flight. This being the second trip to pick up a new grandmother in the last week, I was feeling pretty confident. In all the swirl of the new baby's arrival, here was one thing that I could do well—drive and deliver. My adventurous mom has visited me in Chicago, San Francisco and Munich, Germany, over the years, as study and work took me to new cities. The year after Munich, she went to Hungary with her church for Habitat for Humanity. But none of those adventures matched the anticipation of today and the meeting with her first grandchild.

She had taken the first flight out of Dallas, and with the two hours gained in time zones, it was still early on a brilliant California morning in May. We parked in front of our house and walked around to the back, opening the door quietly, not sure if Jackson was awake or asleep taking his morning nap. We heard voices from the living room and made our way towards them.

"Well hi, Ginny! How was your flight?" Barbara walked across the room and greeted my mom with a hug.

"Hi Barbara, it's so good to see you. My flight was fine……" She was saying the words, but as she released the hug, my mom's eyes were on Marisa who was sitting on the couch holding Jack.

"Come on over here and sit down next to your new grandson, Ginny," Marisa said, grinning. "Here's a little fellow who wants to meet his other grandma."

I watched my mom sit down on the green couch next to Marisa and receive Jackson into her arms. He was swaddled in his morning garb, snugly wrapped up but awake and looking about at all the commotion. He looked up at his newest grandma and arched his back and stretched. His two little feet broke free of the swaddle and his little toes wriggled happily.

Hi, Grandma! I imagined him thinking. *Look what I can do!*

"Oh, isn't he precious. You forget just how tiny they are." Again, her words were for us, but her focus was all on little Jack. "Oh Marisa, he's just perfect."

We passed the day with sandwiches and stories, dishwashing and diapers. It felt good to have both moms in the house. Last year, Marisa had arranged a Moms' Weekend in Sedona, Arizona, to bring both grandmas together to get to know each other. Barbara and Ginny had hit it off like college girlfriends reunited again with tales to tell. To me at the time, it had just been another one of my wife's big ideas—Marisa lives for planning vacations. The first day of any vacation, she will always spend time brainstorming the next vacation. It amazes me every time. "Shouldn't we be enjoying this one, here now?" my brain always asks. But tonight, as I sit in a quiet house with three sleeping mothers and one new grandson, I look back on the Sedona weekend event and see how glad I am Marisa planned it.

During the afternoon's activities today, I had a quiet moment with my mom and I thanked her for flying out and being with us.

"Oh Dylan, it's just a treasure to be here. This is what women have been doing since forever, helping out the new mommy, so the new mommy can help out the baby. I'm just happy to be invited, and to be welcomed and be present."

My mom has an inner strength that I've wondered about my entire life. She smiles and she deflects and she acts coy, but underneath all of that, there is a direction about her, an aura of constancy, focus and strength, unwavering in her love and attention. As much as I've learned to be a man by watching my father, I've learned to be a person by watching my mom.

Mom's coming more clearly into view the older I get. I'm lucky to have her and I know I'm blessed. And I know that I married a tiger mommy, too. I know that Marisa is fierce. I am grateful to be her partner for this life, like I know my dad is grateful for my mom. I know my mom held our family together, and I know that my Marisa will hold our family together, no matter what life has in store for us.

I'm glad my mom's here in the house with us tonight, sharing in Jackson's ninth day of life and in the miracle that has become our life as a family.

13 — May 7, 2007

Our son is 13 days old today. We took Paul Jackson Bonaventure to the doctor's office for his two week checkup. He's gained 14 ounces above his birth weight and is a happy, healthy, 9 pound, 6 ounce baby boy.

After seeing our new pediatrician, we came out to find a parking ticket on the car, a little Los Angeles hello from the meter maid. Grandma G was with us, and little Jack's check-up was good, so it didn't seem so bad.

I talked to my cousin Charlie today and compared baby notes. Charlie, who was a bachelor groomsman at my wedding, is now married and has a 6 month old in his home too, so we were able to share ideas and observations.

Over Labor Day weekend of 2004, the year after Marisa and I married, Charlie and Betty swung by the Spunky Flats ranch and paid an unexpected house call on my dad and mom. A few hours later, I'd gotten a call from Mom.

"Well guess what just happened here this afternoon?" Mom began. "Your cousin Charlie stopped by with Betty. They were on their way to San Antonio for their... honeymoon!"

"They'd gotten married?" I asked.

"Not exactly. They showed up here with a marriage certificate all signed and ready to go. There were looking for Preacher Jack. They were eloping."

"You're kidding."

"Nope. We all got up and went out into the Aggie Acre and picked a grove of trees down where the hill starts to slope to stand under. Your father happened to have his <u>Book of Common Worship</u> in his things here at the ranch so he presided from that. I was the witness and *Dottie Girl* waited patiently at our feet, with—get this—her Frisbee in her mouth. One more special moment at Spunky Flats."

My now-married cousin Charlie's got great perspective on things, and I love catching up with him. He's also funny. He used to brag about never touching a diaper in his life. I think that is changing for him now.

I left messages for recovery friends this evening and got a couple of call-backs. One friend told me that he still checks to make sure his son is breathing every time he looks in on him, and his son is two years old. It made me feel like I'm not crazy.

I went in to work today, even though I am still officially on leave. I needed some space out of the house. I also needed a haircut, and there's a cheap place on campus. I had been thinking of a haircut for a while and it couldn't be put off any longer. I let my hair get shaggy for Jack's birth, my back-to-nature impulse.

And, I needed to reassure myself about work. As much as I want to be peaceful and present to supporting Marisa and Jack, my worries about work still creep into my head. This is the busiest part of our year for admission applications and I'm not in the office and I needed to reassure myself that things are okay. The team was just fine.

I'm sitting on the foot of the bed looking up at my wife and son. She's just fed him and he's looking around, kind of Muppet-like. He continues to be a big eater. We have talked to lots of parents now and learned of so many different challenges that can happen with infants. At least in the eating department, we are not having any trouble. When he collapses his neck, his cheeks spread out, and he gets very narrow, line-like eyes. I call him *pumpkin, bumpkin*, all those kind of names. Sometimes, he'll knit his brow when we talk to him or move him around.

I love this tiny person. Sometimes I wonder: *Who are we going to raise him to be? What is the gift he will bring to life?* His presence. Yes. For sure, that is who he is. His being here is a present.

That's My First Grandson... — May 10, 2007

...is what my mother said to the large, bored baggage attendant at LAX, her voice cracking. She pointed to Jack in the car as she checked in at curbside, getting her flight back to Texas after a week's visit with us. I could hear her through the open car window as we pulled away. Talking to the baggage guy, she was happy and almost crying at the same time. I had to focus on driving or I would be sad and crying at Mom's leaving.

In the backseat, Marisa was weepy, too, driving home after dropping off her mother-in-law. Weepy because they have a great relationship, weepy because both grandmas have come and gone, and now we're on our own. No more hospital, no more grandmas. Weepy because that is what you do in this chapter of being a new mom. You weep.

Two hours later, I get a phone call from Dad. "Where's Momma?" he asks abruptly, not hiding his annoyance. My dad's at the airport in Dallas waiting for my mother's flight to arrive, a flight that's running late. He misses my mom when they're apart, and he doesn't like airports anymore since 9/11. So standing in an airport, late at night, for a late flight, when his wife's been away for over a week, makes him irritable.

We talk. He calms and all is well. When we hang up, I take a cell phone photo of Marisa and Jack and send it to his telephone, so he can see his grandson while he's waiting for his wife. He calls back, now joyful at getting the photo.

I spoke with my brother Jon, too, who's someone I can always count on to lift my spirits. Jon's one of those happy people, and I'm in the mood for some of that happiness tonight.

We sent out birth announcements yesterday. Marisa loves them, a large photo of Jack's face at the top, then three filmstrip-like shots of him in black and white below.

I changed him then burped him. He nursed for an hour. That's the longest he's fed since we were in the hospital. I burped him for ten minutes and thought he was asleep. But when I put him down flat in the crib, he started burping up milk. So I cleaned him and held him some more. He then got the hiccups so I started stroking his head with my free hand and that seemed to soothe him. The hiccups disappeared right after that.

We noticed he got agitated tonight when Marisa started to feed him while within earshot of an episode of *ER* on TV. Makes sense. That show often upsets me, and I'm a fully grown adult.

The first visit of a first-time grandma. Wow. That was a big deal.

My mom left today, announcing to anyone who'd listen that she'd just seen her first ever grandson. Her younger sister, my aunt, recently became a great grandmother and has now been a grandmother for almost 30 years. My mom has waited patiently for a long time to become a grandma. At her church, there is a grandmother's club, and she finally gets to join. It is a big deal for her, too.

The two grandmothers' visits overlapped for a few days, and then my mom stayed on after Barbara left. The two of them got along great. They each have their own biological sisters. I don't know if that helps, or if they just happen to click. Either way, it was great having them here.

The only challenge happened the first day my mom arrived. Barbara smelled gas in the house, so she and Marisa called the gas company. Our house is over 70 years old, so it wasn't surprising when the gas man found two small leaks. The leaks have been there for the three years we've lived here, but we never noticed it. Grandma Szem has a good nose! The challenge came when we had no hot water since the gas company had to shut off the gas water heater while we waited for a plumber. Two grandmas, one wife and one brand new baby, and no hot water—I was afraid it was going to be a disaster. We got a plumber the next day who capped off the two leaks, and we were able to turn the gas back on to restore the hot water. Disaster averted.

Barbara and Ginny helped us get the baby's car seat installed properly by taking it to the Highway Patrol. They got lost driving Marisa's car and had a grand adventure driving around in circles underneath the LA overpasses. My mom always has adventures traveling. My mom always gets off a plane ride with wonderful stories about the person who sat next to her. She smiles and listens, and people tell her all kinds of things about themselves.

Having both grandmas here was special. We talked and hung out, like a big kids' slumber party. Marisa got all the support, advice and comfort food she could handle. Each mom took turns cooking, and the aroma of home cooked meals filled the house and brought back great memories of my childhood.

My mom took ten years away from her teaching career to stay home and raise me, my sister and brother. As a family, we rarely ate out in the 70s, so her cooking was what nourished us for our entire childhood. Even though having Jack is making me feel like more of a grown up than ever, having Mom here supporting us and cooking was like replaying a small slice of my childhood. Sharing Barbara's cooking gave me a peek into Marisa's youth.

Mom did all the helpful things this week. She didn't offer advice unless asked directly for it, and even then, I had to beg for it. She is a big believer in boundaries, and sometimes I have to drag an opinion out of her. She made us feel like we were doing great, even when we didn't know what we were doing. She offered unlimited encouragement.

The two grandmas are now home in South Carolina and Texas, respectively. We are here. I can't imagine being a new father with any other type of grandmotherly love than what I received from both grandmas these last two weeks. Jack is sleeping and Marisa, too. Milestones. These are big ones that I don't ever want to forget.

Daddy Diapers — May 14, 2007

Here's the deal. If I want to get some baby-time with my newborn, I gotta learn how to do the diaper thing better than anybody. Marisa, she has a whole lot of other things to do with the little person: feeding, cuddling, dressing, all the good stuff. So, what's that leave for Poppa?

1) Holding him while he's crying.

2) Taking photos of mommy doing everything with him.

3) Changing those diapers.

When my wonderful son was born, I'd probably held small babies for a total of 30 minutes over my entire life. Nothing like forgetting to practice before the big game. So on April 25, 2007, a few short hours after Jack was born, I started my on-the-job diaper change training.

It began that first night in the hospital. Everything that came out of newborn Jack looked like gluey spinach paste—greenish black and sticky. It was 4 a.m., and I thought desperately... *18 years of this?* Thankfully, I realized that I'd never seen a teenager in diapers, so it couldn't possibly last that long. My goal was to get the old diaper off, clean up the mess, and get the new diaper on straight, before the little rocket could launch a new fountain of pee in every direction.

We had Jack sleeping on his back in his crib. SIDS Alert! Let's all freak out about SIDS. SIDS is *Sudden Infant Death Syndrome*, a terrible thing that can happen to young children. About 1 out of 2,000 infants will just suddenly die while lying asleep in their cribs. It's horrible. The cause is not known for sure, but they tell us that keeping baby on his back will help prevent SIDS.

I am learning to know when it is diaper changing time. The diaper gets big. It gets warm. There is a smell. So when it's time, I pick up Jack and bring him to the changing table. Yes, a table is best, someplace where I can work without hunching over, where I can peer down and do my splendid diaper surgery. Good lighting, tools at the ready, maybe a CD player close with some *muzak-de-pooh-pooh*.

All the infant clothes have little snaps. I find the crotch snaps and pull back his *über*-cute outfit to reveal the masterpiece that is the modern newborn diaper. How did people deal with this in the Middle Ages? How about pioneers in covered wagons? I'm dumbfounded wondering about old fashioned diapers. No wonder men went out and hunted. Wild animals with teeth had to be an easier challenge than primitive diapers. Dealing with modern, convenient diapers is bad enough, but I can't even imagine it in earlier times.

Jack likes to stretch when he's on the changing table. He's adorable when he arches his back and rolls his head, sticking his chin out. He raises his eyebrows while keeping his eyes closed—a wiggle worm and I love it. And I learned all that stretching leads to farting, a few trumpet blasts, if I am patient. I tickle him and gently squeeze his round little tummy, hoping to adjust his insides, so he'll go longer without needing to change diapers again.

He looks up during the blissful stretching and I get to see two big eyes, eyes that still don't see me, but worth it every time. Next comes removing the old diaper. Two self-adhesive tabs open up and fold down, like post-it notes with just enough cling. The puffed up front of the diaper is full of liquid, doing its job. I peel it back to see what I have to contend with in the cleanup department.

In the hospital, we had to log everything we found in our own special poop and pee journal. Was there pee? Was there poop? Was there pee and poop? Like a National Geographic explorer, all these encounters went into our little notebook, one of those combinations every time.

The black-green glue-paste only lasted the first two days. Then there was a downtime while mom produced colostrum. Colostrum comes from the breast before the actual breast milk arrives, flowing for about the first three days. This helps baby get used to nursing, and then the real breast milk comes in.

Over the first two months of diapering, I learned a few other tricks. My buddy Steve from Denison is the father of two pre-teen sons, and he taught me how to wrap the used diaper back into itself, compacted into a tiny little ball. I learned to keep a camera and a video camera at the ready, as diaper time was full of magic smiles. I ordered a 1970s CD, *Free to Be, You and Me,* and listened to it during diaper time. We'd had it on a vinyl album when I was a kid. It was funny how the CD somehow left the diaper area and ended up in my car, with me blasting cheery children's music on the way to work.

They say the *past* is a memory, the *future* is a maybe, and *now* is all we have. It's a gift and that is why it is called the present. Watching little bumpkin make his faces and arch his back and wiggle on the changing table, I started to get the gift that is diaper time.

Personal Email — May 15, 2007

From: Dylan Stafford, Director of Admissions

Sent: Tuesday, May 15, 2007 12:26 PM

To: All Faculty, All Staff, All FEMBA and EMBA Students

Subject: Personal Email - Birth of our first child

Dear UCLA Anderson Faculty, Staff, and Students,

Please forgive this purely personal communication, but it describes the best experience of my life, which I want to share with all of you. Our first child was born on April 25, at 1:30 a.m. at UCLA Medical Center in Westwood. His birth was an emergency c-section, and both baby and Mom are doing great. Paul Jackson Bonaventure Stafford arrived in the world weighing 8 pounds, 8 ounces, and was 21 inches long.

I want to thank the faculty, staff and students of UCLA Anderson who support our admission efforts. Thank you for all the support as this amazing life chapter is unfolding for our family.

My vision of the future includes organizations that work for everyone, that create great products and services, and also bring out the best in their employees, so those employees go home at the end of the day with energy for their families and society. I'm inspired knowing our graduates take this type of leadership around the country and around the world. It's an honor to work here.

With appreciation,

Dylan Stafford - Director of Admissions,

UCLA Anderson School - Fully Employed MBA + Executive MBA

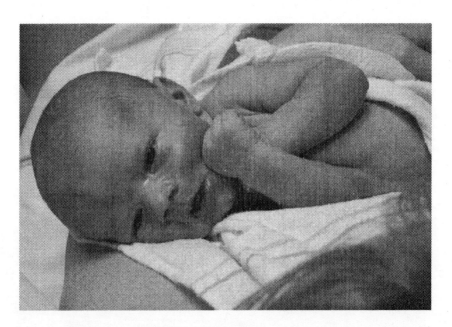

PS   Paul Jackson Bonaventure Stafford

Paul honors my wife's father. Jackson honors my father. Bonaventure honors the band U2's music, Bono's efforts in third world debt relief, and St. Bonaventure.

Nanny Interviews — June 16, 2007

I am not the only father to have bold ideas when his first child is born, not the only father to think about turning over a new leaf in honor of the miracle his wife made happen. For me, my new leaf was that I was going to write stories like this one. I was going to put into print my experience of being a new dad. It's now been almost five weeks since I last wrote about our new son, our Paul Jackson Bonaventure Stafford.

Five weeks and no writing, am I failing at this already?

Across the bed, Jack is on my wife's lap. She's whispering to him while he sleeps. And her reward for whispering is that he wakes up and cries loudly. I love this little guy. He'll be 8 weeks old in two days. We have used up half of Marisa's maternity leave and it is freaking me out thinking that soon she won't be able to stay home anymore with Jack. As vulnerable as I felt when grandma left, it's going to be ten times worse after maternity leave ends. I have an impending doom feeling about who is going to take care of him when she goes back to work. We don't have that figured out.

He's not a pet, our little baby son. We can't leave him in the kitchen overnight on a bunch of spread-out newspapers and clean up in the morning. We can't put him in the backyard for the afternoon and go see a movie. He's a helpless, totally dependent, little human being. He needs us for everything: food, shelter, clothes, cleaning, loving. It's a lot.

We interviewed a potential caregiver tonight, a nice middle aged woman. She's from Mexico originally, but she told us, "I have a license and a car and insurance. A lot of ladies drive without a license." Here in Los Angeles everyone says *nanny*, but to me we are talking about a babysitter, not a nanny. To me, a nanny is someone who lives in with the family and is there full time, like Julie Andrews in *The Sound of Music*. I never had a nanny when I was a kid, only babysitters from the family across the street or people from church. We were a small town preacher's family. My mom took ten years out of her teaching career and raised her three kids. A nanny? Not in our family. Probably not in our whole town, but here in Los Angeles, nanny it is.

How do we decide something like this? Of all the millions of people in Los Angeles, how do we find the one person who will take care of Jack? This is the part of Los Angeles life that I hate. Everything here seems so big to me. Everything is such a production. Am I just a small town Texas kid at heart? Do I not have what it takes to succeed here? At first Los Angeles seems easy with the palm trees and the beach, like in the movies. But that's the sexy tourist view on things. To actually live here is expensive, and we don't have our family with us here. Sometimes I feel like we are one slip away from disaster.

I have never felt as vulnerable as I feel this summer. Marisa is being the Super Mommy now, and Jack is in perfect care. But what happens when she has to go back to work? We don't know how we will care for Jack when that happens.

Marisa walked Jack around to the nanny circle in the park across from our house, checking out the group of dark-haired Hispanic women caring for all these blond Caucasian kids. She introduced herself and started getting to know the different caregivers. She noticed who was nice to little Jackson and who was indifferent. She saw who was always chatting on their cell phone, not paying as much attention their charges.

We are interviewing for someone to take care of Jack when maternity leave ends, to be in our home with him while we go to work. The easy part of the problem is that we can't afford it, since they charge $15 an hour, which would be $600 a week, which is too much. The hard part of the problem is what happens if something goes wrong? What if there is an accident? As good as they may be, they aren't Marisa the Super Mommy.

My real fear is how do I know if we can trust them? What if someone takes Jack and flees, to another city, to another country? That's the first thought I had on contemplating a nanny—*What if we came home one night and Jack is gone?* Where would we begin? "Hello, police. Our son is gone. He is with a woman, Hispanic..." That would not narrow it down very much in Los Angeles. How crazy would that be? My brain is picking the worst possible outcome, but I can't help it. I hate this vulnerable feeling. I feel like a real father would never allow a situation where his family could even possibly be exposed. I feel like I've failed already, my whole life inadequate to the task of taking care of our baby.

Marisa found one nanny who seemed to be all business with the children in her care. She made goo-goo eyes at Jackson and complimented Marisa on how big he was. They seemed to connect and Marisa continued talking to her for several days, which led to our interview tonight.

There's a big debate in Congress and the press right now over amnesty and what the U.S should do to legally manage the flow of people coming here from Mexico and Central America. Close the Border & Send 'em Home, vs. Make 'em legal & Give Us your Tired, your Poor, your Hungry. The two sides do battle on cable TV and talk radio. I didn't think the issue had much to do with me until today, while sitting in our living room talking to a woman whose family story was similar to the people making the news. Something big and national suddenly became small and personal.

We have been calling local child care facilities, too. In West Los Angeles, child care is a big issue with too much demand and not enough supply.

You have to pay money even to place your name on the waiting lists. We paid our waitlist deposits at UCLA and several places before Jack was born, even before we told our parents we were pregnant. That is how much demand there is.

Our goal is to keep Jack home until he is one year old, since that is how long it takes to come off a waitlist, we are told. Doing the math, it means we would need eight months of nanny care in our home. It is going to cost a fortune. How is this going to work? And even more troubling, what if we make a mistake and choose the wrong person to care for our precious Jack?

I'm feeling like a failure. If I were a real bread-winner, and made enough money to support this family, we could afford all of this. Maybe if I had stayed with engineering and chosen a better career path, we would have better options. Maybe Marisa wouldn't have to go back to her job so soon, she could take a year off. Some of my roommates from Texas A&M, Jeff and Brady, have been able to do that with their families. I shouldn't compare myself, but I do anyway, and I always come up short. I feel like everything I have done for my 38 years of life is not enough for the task of being Jack's dad and parent and taking care of him and Marisa. My dad did better than this. He did it with three children, and I'm feeling like I can't manage with one.

We have two months to figure this out.

First Father's Day — June 18, 2007

Yesterday was my first Father's Day. I didn't feel like it applied to me. It felt like people were wishing me Merry Christmas, but I was secretly Jewish.

"Happy Father's Day."

"Thanks," I replied, thinking to myself, *I'm not really technically a father. Fathers are much older men, like my dad.* I'm not sure how many times the greeting was wished on me before it started to sink in that it applied to me, too.

All three of us went to church for the first time yesterday. On Mother's Day, Marisa had gone in alone, and I had kept Jackson with me and gone grocery shopping. We weren't ready yet for so many people putting their fingerprints on him. That day the church did a big appreciation of all the mothers, giving them each a carnation and inviting them all to the front of the church for an acknowledgement. Marisa came out with eyes wet from happy crying with a giant satisfied smile on her face.

But on Father's Day, we three were ready. We started packing at 11 a.m., for the 1:15 p.m. service. Would we make it on time? We had to think about when to feed him. Should we have a spare bottle? Was the diaper bag fully stocked? Was the binky clean and available? Should we take the stroller or the car seat? Would there be a parking spot in the shade? Should we bring a spare outfit? If there is such thing as a patience muscle, mine is getting a workout every day.

We all three went inside. We carried our little love in to the back corner of the church.

"Is he your first?" whispered an older woman.

"Yes, he is our first."

"You should have another one."

In my Father's Day service, unlike Marisa on Mother's Day, I didn't go to the front when they called all the dads forward. I was holding Jackson, and I didn't want to disturb him. We had carried him in our arms without the portable cradle. I was so proud holding him. I made eye contact with lots of other dads. It was funny the way we dads acknowledged each other, acting surprised that there were so many of us. It was as if we should exchange phone numbers to get together. We didn't. After the service everyone split off to go into their respective directions. Maybe some dads met with each other, but I followed my wife and listened to her talking to a woman whose husband wasn't there—"He had to work"—and whose son was three weeks older than Jackson, but much smaller.

****

I am sitting here in the evening writing. Marisa has put Paul Jackson down for a few minutes, so she could go into the other room to pump. Her goal is to breastfeed him for at least his first year. She pumps and stores the extra milk for when we're in public and breastfeeding isn't convenient.

"He may start crying. If he does, please go to him." Those are my instructions.

It's 9:27 p.m. and I'm exhausted. It's only Monday, for goodness sake. What am I, *elderly*? When my son is 21, I will be 59. That's kind of elderly-in-the-making. Maybe I *should* be tired. At least I live in a city where there will be lots of older parents. Los Angeles has plenty of "old" new parents like us.

Marisa did the coolest thing. Last night, at the end of the evening, I looked at my pillow on the bed, and there were two cards placed against it.

"Which should I open first?" I asked, and she told me to open the white one. It was my first Father's Day Card. It was from her and it was lovely. Then I opened the second one, and it was my second Father's Day Card, but it was from Jack. It was Marisa's writing, but it was Jack's voice thanking me for being his daddy.

Happy Father's Day, Daddy.…..

Fatherhood—it's happening for me, too.

Daddy Muscles — July 3, 2007

Judy's Cabin, Estes Park, Colorado

We're on the first leg of our summer vacation, traveling for the first time with our new son. I'm sitting on the porch of a red cabin in Estes Park, Colorado, looking out at Long's Peak and the high country in Rocky Mountain National Park while Marisa and Jack take an afternoon nap. It's rained here and the air is cool and pine tree fresh. A humming bird is busy outside sipping nectar from a feeder, oblivious of me.

Being a new father has me think often of my own childhood. When I was a teenager, I thought having muscles was somehow connected to getting the girl. I'd exercise. I'd roll up my sleeves to get a tan to show off my teenage guns. I'd do pushups before I went on a date. My younger sister Lisa would see me out on the back porch, staring at the floor with a bead of sweat on my nose as I got pumped up. She'd laugh and laugh. Those shoulder, arm and chest muscles seemed so very important back then. How could I ever attract a wonderful-beautiful girlfriend without them?

I'm not a teenager anymore. I'm 38 years old now, and my wife and I have our first baby—ten weeks old tomorrow—our little miracle son Jack. But he's got me thinking about muscles again.

On Father's Day, when we took him to his first church service, the organ started and church began. Jack slept most of the time and we only stepped out once when I thought he might start crying. I held my son in my

162

arms for that entire church service. It was the longest I'd ever held him at one sitting since usually mommy has him. Those long muscles in the middle of my back started to ache. They hurt to the point where I rocked my back against the hard wooden pew to relieve them, while trying to keep Jack sleeping. I could have handed him back to my wife of course, but she was looking at me like a hero and holding him was something I could do for her.

And at church, to be a new father holding his new son is to be a very special person. People smiled at me—and beamed at him. Other fathers made eye contact and gave me the subtle nod. So, aching back or not, there was nothing I wanted to do but to keep holding him.

It's similar when we're back at the house, carrying, burping, and moving with him. I get out of the chair, bend over the crib, circle the park, lock the car seat, squat for the dropped pacifier. All of these actions are taken with our now 10 pound, ever-growing bundle of joy in my arms.

My wife has all the baby books stacked by our bed, but I haven't read any of them and now that I'm writing this book, it makes me laugh—do guys even read about babies? If I were to read one, I bet there'd be a chapter about *don't drop the baby*, seems like they would make a big deal about that. So all that bending and squatting with a baby has to be done just right. I can't get it wrong. I have to balance. I can't get fatigued. I have to smile and coo and show love, even when I am tired and frustrated.

Getting frustrated is definitely part of all it. Even though Marisa does most of everything, and it feels like I don't have any right to complain, I still get frustrated. *I want what I want when I want it*, between recovery and Landmark, I've learned all about that character flaw of mine. Jack is changing all that. He cries. He eats. He needs attention. All on his time table, not mine. There are so many little changes that go along with the big change of the new baby entering our life.

One example of my frustration is not knowing how to respond when my wife asks me, "Do you think he might be hungry?" It's an easy question. It's an important question, but really, our little monster eats every 2-3 hours—*all day long*. If he's awake, he's hungry. Still my wife asks. I'll hear the hunger question all through the day.

Holding my tongue, now that's another new muscle that is getting a workout. I have to slow down and remind myself that we've never done this before. And, at the same time, it's the most important thing we've ever done. Our son is 100% dependent on us for his food and clothing and shelter. Does it make sense to monitor his feeding schedule religiously? Of course it does.

Patience, baby-holding, tongue-holding—all are developing strong muscles that can't be seen from the outside. My back muscles may be getting stronger, but no one can see. I try to pause and not be so selfish, another muscle I'm developing that can't be seen either. I call these new strengths that life asks of new fathers *daddy muscles*. Pregnancy lasts 40 weeks, and Mommy's body grows stronger that whole time. But I have a hunch that Mommy started building her muscles long before that. She had a lifetime of watching and thinking and preparing for being a Mommy.

Daddy? Pretty sure Daddy wasn't paying too much attention. Before we got married, Marisa would ask me, "What kind of wedding have you always imagined?" Somehow she was underwhelmed with the blank stare that greeted her question. Well, I was a lot like that about being a father, too. All I knew, mostly from the movies, was that it had to somehow stay in balance. Too much work and you are a bad daddy—the "Cat's in the Cradle with the Silver Spoon" problem. Not enough work, and you're a bad daddy. But beyond that to specifics like diapers and feeding schedules and bedtimes… just a blank stare.

I had a *concept* of being a father from my own experience of being a son. I imagined trips with grandpa to the central Texas family ranch, or summer vacations in Colorado, teaching fishing and hammering and sawing and nailing and digging holes. That's what being a Daddy meant to me. Not much more, certainly not changing diapers and all the other heavy lifting.

When she was pregnant, Marisa didn't really show until five and a half months. She didn't have a lot of the morning sickness, either. So while we talked about being pregnant, it didn't disrupt our lives too much in the first half of the 40 weeks.

Those 40 weeks are important. Mommy's muscles are growing, but Daddy's muscles have to start growing, too. Seems like that's why babies are so small when they're born. It takes time to build those muscles. We've got to start small and exercise, just like the pushups I did as a teenager long ago. Only now, it's not about getting the girl. It's not even about keeping the girl, really. Marisa and I have stood in front of God and everybody, and made a vow that we are in this, together, for the rest of our lives.

Now it is about being a Daddy. Loving Mommy and being there for our little pumpkin. It's about strength for that journey, the muscles to make that trip.

Rocky Mountain High ~ Grandpa — July 10, 2007

We're visiting the northeast now, New Jersey and Boston, the second leg of our summer vacation to visit family after leaving Colorado. Yesterday morning, my son got hit with his first raindrop. It was a big, wet drop, and it landed right on his arm. He didn't cry. He didn't even seem to notice it.

Los Angeles is in drought and it's only rained a total of four inches the last year, but it's raining now in this Boston suburb where we are staying, a steady shower all morning. When the rain ended, I stepped out onto the patio of Patty and Michael's home—Patty, Marisa's maid of honor and herself the mother of two sons. Our Jackson had been crying, so I took him outside to see if the contrast would distract him and calm him down.

"Look at the trees," I said, moving out into the yard. "Look at the sky."

Plop. Wet arm.

A big dollop of a splattered raindrop now sat on Jack's forearm but at least he wasn't crying anymore. It was so hot and humid that he didn't get cold like he does at bath time. I went back inside with a calm son.

"He just got rained on for the first time ever," I said with enthusiasm, as I handed Jack over to my wife. Marisa looked him over sharply, making sure I hadn't brought our boy back dripping wet from his outdoor adventure.

"That's great," she said, assured no damage was done.

Our two week, three-state trip, is full of firsts for the Stafford family. We rode in a plane together for the first time. Jack saw both his grandfathers, each for the first time. We left California, visited Colorado, and now New Jersey and Massachusetts. All firsts. We've been meeting cousins. Before Saturday, Jack had never met any, and now he has met all eight of his Jersey cousins.

At each stop along the way, we get out of the rental car, we stretch and Marisa gathers her things. I go to the trunk and strap a diaper bag around my shoulder, then come and liberate the car seat with Jack still in it, and, carrying the whole package, accompany Marisa to our next visit. People kiss the baby, showering him with love and attention. Digital cameras appear and flicker. We usually have at least one diaper change on someone's living room floor or couch. He's the new baby to be passed around and loved—grandbaby number nine on my wife's side, and grandbaby number one on mine.

Last week in Colorado, my father got to meet his first grandchild in his favorite place on earth, the Rocky Mountains. We flew into Denver and then drove the two hours up to Estes Park to meet my parents at the red cabin where they spent their honeymoon in 1965. The cabin is a family place owned by Dad's high school buddy, and also best man at his wedding, Marvin. Majestic Ponderosa Pines stand sentinel over the granite gravel driveway in the back, while on the other side, the front porch windows stare straight at Longs Peak, the tallest point in Rocky Mountain National Park. Under those same Ponderosa Pines in an early 60s college summer, Dad has a photo of himself and Marvin next to the motorcycles they had ridden 900 miles from Dallas, both men and trees over 40 years thinner.

Dad was a rebel in his way, being in his 30s during my childhood years, vital and alive and inspiring to me. He lost an early preaching job in east Texas, for accompanying some black ministers to the bank to discuss fair hiring practices. There are pictures of him from the early 70s with a big bushy head of Jim Croce hair and massive lamb chop sideburns. In my mind, my dad is always, eternally about 39. He's just mowed the backyard and is sweaty and strong, and the biggest guy in the world, sitting at the head of the table as we say grace before dinner.

Dad was my hero each summer when we took our family vacation in the Colorado backcountry. Those vacations were Dad's deal, his to make the plans for, picking the location, the time of year, the activities. He'd say when we'd make the drive up to Colorado, when we'd pitch our tent, make the fire to cook or set up the Coleman stove, and when we'd go to town for showers, all of it. I rode in the back of our VW bus, reading The Hobbit and imagining the mysteries of the mountains.

Those summer vacations were magical to me. Dad was in such a good mood before vacations. Germans have a saying about anticipation being the best joy. Dad anticipated and savored the vacation and the preparation, and it was contagious to be around him. He taught me about passion, not by saying a word, but by how alive he would be during those many summer months over my childhood that we had together.

Jackson cried during part of the drive from Denver, as the altitude changed and his ears adjusted. We arrived and pulled up to the red cabin, the first destination of our vacation. We shut off the car, got out, and stretched. The sound of chairs scooching along the old linoleum floor could be heard through the wall, as my parents got up from the kitchen table and came outside to greet us.

All morning, on the plane ride from Los Angeles and the curvy drive into the mountains, I'd been anticipating this moment. While Marisa was exchanging hugs on the other side of the car, I unlatched the car seat and picked up a wide-eyed Paul Jackson.

"Bring him over," Marisa called to me.

It's strange that I didn't really watch my dad's initial reaction to meeting his grandson. I was so curious all morning, but in that moment, I found myself looking at my son instead of looking to see my dad's expression. It was as if I didn't want to intrude. I wanted them to have their own communication without my interruption.

My dad is 64 years old and he's waited a long time to become a grandpa. My mom waited a long time, too. I used to tease her about it, "Mom, remember when you used to ask me, 'Are you dating any *nice* girls?' And then you changed it to, 'Are you dating *any* girls?' with the *nice* dropped out." It wasn't quite that bad. Both my parents were actually very patient and encouraging while I went through my 20s and early 30s before I finally settled down.

As if he were receiving a brim-full glass of red wine while standing on a white carpet, my dad gently, carefully received his grandson into his arms. We weren't on a white carpet, but rather on the gravel where my young beanpole father took that college photo with Marvin and the motorcycles over 40 years earlier, standing under these same Ponderosa Pines. Grandma G was seeing Jack for the second time. Grandpa was seeing and holding him for the first time, and as I watched Dad, I wondered how long it had been since he'd held an infant. I wondered what it was like for him to remember holding me when I was that size. I wondered what it would be like for me to hold my own grandbaby someday and remember back to holding Jack. It's all been done a billion times before, fathers and sons linked over the eons, and yet, it's the first time for me, for my dad, and his first grandson.

Yesterday, on Interstate 95 between Massachusetts and New Jersey, Marisa was talking about not mixing up the process with the person. She meant, in the process of caring for the baby, it's important not to forget the actual baby, that he is having his own experience, too. It made sense to me. I'm writing these daddy diaries to capture all the firsts and seconds of Jack's life, and asking, *what's it like for the baby?* I'm also asking about our process: *What's it like for us, the parents, grandparents, family and friends?* In the greater experience, I see how it does take a village. As a dad, I've been surrounded by village a lot more than I had realized. Before Jack, I thought I was so unique, doing things in such an independent manner.

But all that is changing, the further we progress into parenthood. We really are all connected. We can't raise this baby by ourselves. We need resources, support, wisdom and love. And people are ready to offer all that and more. People love babies. It's a cliché, but it's true.

Weddings bring out people's *good*. At weddings, people get happy and they aren't afraid to show it. But babies bring out people's *best*. People flat out gush for babies. It's humbling, as I vainly consider myself a charismatic guy who speaks often to large groups of people, but I can't create the reaction Jack creates. Our little two month old baby might as well be a rock star. When he enters the room, people spring out of their chairs. They abandon their normal slow sensations and *move*. They make weird noises and strange faces—talk about audience reaction! I'll never be able to match the charisma of a little, tiny baby.

It is amazing. He's bringing out my best, too. I find myself wanting to get organized, like a real grown-up, to lead and direct my life in a new way, to speak up and speak out. The *someday* I've always dreamed about, the time to be who I really am, has arrived. The warm-up is over and the game has begun!

During our visits this week, I've shared some of these daddy diaries. There have been a few attaboys, even some tears—imagine me, a rainmaker. Sharing what I have been writing is like giving a gift. This is why I am writing. Maybe I really can do this.

Baby Ache — July 12, 2007

Chocolate eyes. My baby's eyes are brown, but doesn't *chocolate* sound more exciting? Some of his cousins have brown eyes, some have blue. It was fun last week, visiting Jack's eight cousins and having everyone meet each other. Marisa's sister Bonnie has two boys, Craig and Connor, who both have blue eyes, while her daughter Carly got brown eyes. Bonnie and Marisa are both light-eyed, and they both married dark-eyed chocolatiers, Gary and me.

I went to a church meeting tonight. It was an educational session for everyone involved in the upcoming baptism ceremony. Baptism marks the receipt of a gift, which is a new life and a new spirit. Many Christians don't even know about the gift of baptism, according to our priest who was speaking tonight. We will be having the Baptism for Paul Jackson one month from today, on August 12. Many of those same cousins are flying out to participate in the ceremony, blue and brown eyes all.

I've been with my wife for two weeks straight, as we finished our vacation today. It's the most I've been around her and our son since the first two weeks when Jack was born. Just leaving Jack for two hours tonight, to go to church and pick up some groceries, made me ache for him when I got back home.

He's asleep already in his crib. He's flat on his back and bent into a sideways C shape. He's not in the little mini-bed within the crib anymore. Over the two weeks we were away, he grew, and now he is big enough to sleep in the crib without the mini-bed. It looks different.

I've been gone two hours and I knew we were going to take out the mini-bed tonight, but still, I come home and see the change and there is an ache in my heart. Like somehow, something important has happened and I have missed it. I don't feel this ache too often. I've worked hard to be present for our little miracle son on a daily basis. So, it catches me off guard to have this baby ache for something missed tonight. We're jetlagged from flying in from New Jersey, and I didn't eat too consistently today. I have a slow, dull, background headache. I thought maybe I was dehydrated, but every time I drink water I feel over-full.

Bottom line is I'm tired and now is not a good time for any melancholy emotions to get in the mix. And it is these times when those emotions always show up. Will we stay in California? Will I keep this job? Those type of questions show up immediately when I feel that baby ache. It's like the homesickness when I go back to Texas and see my family there. Like the baby ache, that homesick ache always makes me think I need to rearrange my life, do something different.

This writing, having stories to share with family and friends, has been an amazing process. Every time I offered to read, it felt like I had homemade chocolate chip cookies to give away. It was something personal and unique that I could offer. It gave us different conversations to have. It made it easier to share my experience of being a dad, more than the back-slapping, new-daddy-Hallmark-card sentiments of *ain't it great* and *I miss my sleep*.

In those two weeks, we were with our village. It may be spread across the country, but it is still our village. The family who raised us is the family we go to as we learn to raise Jack.

I'm truly in love with this little guy who has blessed my life with Marisa. She thanked me for being her husband this week. As we saw her friends and showed off our baby, it dawned on me how rich it is to be married. I *get* to be there for her. I don't have to be rich. I don't have to be clever. I can gain weight. It's not about any of that qualifying stuff I always thought it would be about. It's about being present. It's about being there for her, as her partner.

I talked with my sister Lisa tonight. She's in her new apartment and it's a brand new day in her life. She has a pool she's enjoying, browning up and meeting new people. My sister is one of my heroes. She's a saint in my life. Life is opening up a new chapter for her right now. She met a law professor lately who told her that with her wit she should be writing. How delicious is that? I'm thrilled that she is getting that kind of feedback. She's a great person at a podium, expressing wit when telling a tale. With pen to paper, or fingers to keyboard, there is a world for her to write about.

Lisa was four years behind me in school, a freshman when I was a senior. She is my younger sister, but she is wise and older emotionally than me, many times. In college, when I got dumped by my first real girlfriend, Lisa helped me figure out that ache. She gave me the girl's point of view that I would have never figured out. She helped me through it. Now, Lisa is so curious, learning about Jack and everything we are going through. I have shared some of my daddy diaries with her, and she is always encouraging.

Lisa has chocolate eyes, too. I miss Lisa every time we leave Texas, the same way I miss my parents and brother Jon. If I didn't love people so deeply, then the ache wouldn't be there. I know that in my brain, but when the ache is in my gut and heart, it doesn't matter very much what my brain knows. And now we have added our son Jack. I ache for him when I go away for two hours. All of this is about being alive, being human. It is about raising a little human life. It is about living the life I already had with Marisa. It is a chocolate-ty delicious gift.

Sears Baby Photos — July 25, 2007

On Jack's three month birthday, Marisa and I took him to the Sears portrait studio in Santa Monica. It amazed me that a Sears store still survived on the west side of Los Angeles, where most of the stores are much more upscale. The ubiquitous Wal-Mart doesn't even exist on the west side of Los Angeles. Sears was out of place, but at the same time, it felt right, something familiar in this huge Los Angeles city, something reminding me of my own childhood.

When I was a kid in fifth grade, my brother and I saved our allowance money for a stereo system we wanted to order out of the Sears catalogue. As kids, it was a huge amount of money to us, close to $200. We squirreled away nickels and dimes until we came up with our contribution. We gave the money to Dad, who then matched it and mailed it off to Santa Claus, who somehow managed to come up with the rest.

On a December evening close to Christmas, my brother and I heard jingle bells at the front door, then my father's voice coming from the other room. "Good bye Santa. Thank you, Santa. We love you, Santa." My brother and I ran into the living room where my dad stood at the open front door, calling at Santa who was hurrying on his way to other good little boys and girls.

"You just missed him," Dad said, a twinkle in his eye. I was old enough not to be too distracted by an early visit from Santa Clause and was thrilled to see an enormous cardboard box sitting right in front of the Christmas tree. My little brother was four years younger than me and still fully embraced Santa, so he was bummed at missing him. But he, too, soon became fascinated by the giant box.

(My coffee is poured. Nice. Little Jack is ahhing and quacking from the other room. He's had his breakfast and is lying across mommy's lap, being happy as I sit and write.)

The very first album we played on our new stereo was Billy Joel's *Glass Houses*, the one with "You May Be Right" and all those fast songs. *You may be right, I may be crazy, but it just might be a lunatic you're looking for...* We played that album over and over, dancing to each song around our bedroom. The stereo set had lots of knobs and lights, and the speakers seemed so big. We kept it in our shared bedroom, and I remember how the room would be dark except for the glow from the stereo. The record table would let you stack up to five albums on it at one time. It would play an album, then drop the next album and play it automatically. My brother and I could load five records, get into our bunk beds, and fall asleep listening to the music playing.

My grandpa Harold Dear loved Sears, too. Sears ran in our family. Grandpa Harold Dear used the catalogue to order a patio roof for our house's back porch as a gift to his son. It replaced a lightweight, green fiberglass roof that leaked in places. The night it was delivered, Grandpa drove the 80 miles up from Dallas to oversee the installation. It must have been winter time, because I remember it was already dark when he arrived. My granddad died when I was eight, so my memories of him are all about things that happened when I was a young boy.

Sears came and installed the new patio roof on a blustery, Texas evening. They had to do big manly things with straps and ropes to keep it from lifting up on a gust while they attached it to the mainframe of the house. At one point, the wind did lift one side enough to slam it down with a huge noise. It was an exciting evening for a kid to watch. Grandpa and dad and the crew finally got it bolted down. Mission accomplished, contribution made from father to son, the new patio roof for his grandchildren to play under on the summer days to come.

Now, driving across town in LA traffic on our way to this misplaced Sears, all those memories danced around in my head. I thought about all the families in America over the last 50, 60, 70 years that had made a similar trek with their children to Sears, or to JC Penney, or to some small town portrait studio in the converted room of some guy's house. How many hallways in how many homes were decorated with family photos that resulted from journeys just like this?

Going to Sears with our three month old son made me feel American in the finest sense of the word—loving, family-first, patient, and building for our children's future. That part of what's possible in America. That was the part that was filling me with pride as we drove on our way.

Our appointment to meet the photographer was for 7:00 p.m. When we arrived, there was only one guy working the studio, and he had another family still with him at the computer, cropping and adjusting the images from their just finished photo session. Even Sears is high-tech now.

We waited. Jack started to wail. I walked him all through the electronics section of Sears in his stroller to distract him until our turn came. Twenty minutes later we began. The store was going to close at 8:00 p.m., and the photographer let us know that we couldn't go past 8. *What about the twenty minutes we lost while you worked with that other family?* I thought, but didn't say.

Our photographer was an immigrant to the U.S. He told us his life story while he worked the cameras. He told us his current frustrations with management, plus his real dreams to work in the field of Information Technology. He did this all while adjusting pillows and drapes and snapping photos with those big umbrella lights going *pop* each time he pushed a button.

Jack went along with it pretty well. He sat by himself, propped up on a draped table as we did a lot of parent-jumping-around behind the camera, trying to get a smile to capture for our hallway forever. *Pop, Adjust, Pop.* Parents jump up and down, making silly faces and noises. *Pop, Adjust, Pop.*

Over the next week, Marisa would trek back to Sears two more times to review the results of the photo session and make all the many decisions about number, size, and enhancements. Enhancements were changes to the photos such as selecting black and white, or sepia, or soft lighting. Eight enhancements in all were included in the package, but additional enhancements were always available for only a few dollars more. The photos came out great—large, medium, and small, the whole kit and caboodle. It was worth every silly moment of jumping around like a daddy orangutan to get Jack to smile. Even worth hearing our photographer's lament about how no one appreciates an artist at work anymore.

We proudly shared the finished photos with family. All is well in America. Hallways are decorated and wallets filled. I hope Grandpa Harold Dear, looking down on us from above, is as proud as we are.

Angel Eyes — August 5, 2007

When we hold our son Jack, what do all our ancestors see when they look down from heaven above? Do they mainly see the top of his head? If that were so, then my dad's mom, Bobby Dear, would be cheering wildly, because she is one of the redheads in the family tree who contributed to Jack's hair color—Marisa's mom Barbara is the other. Maybe that's why babies lay on their backs most of the time, so that all the angel eyes up in heaven can get a good look.

This week, while Marisa and I were playing with Jack, I wondered what all our ancestors must think of him. I wondered if they know him already. Did they interview his little soul, or vice versa, before he came to us? When his little soul was looking for a family on earth, did our ancestors sit with him across the table and answer questions about why Marisa and Dylan would be great candidates to consider? Was there any heavenly PowerPoint presentation involved?

I often wonder what my grandfather, Harold Dear, thinks about our little Jack. Grandpa was a lawyer, and after his funeral in 1977 there was a gathering of lawyers who all spoke in tribute to him. It made an impression on me. I was only eight, and it told me that my grandpa was loved and respected, and that I wanted to be like him someday.

When I look at my little son, all of three months and one week old, I think I see a wise soul looking back at me. Do all parents think this? Am I totally reading into his eyes what I want to see? Probably, but that doesn't mean I don't think it.

Do I want our son to make his ancestors proud? You bet I do. Am I also accepting, knowing he will do exactly what he does, and not do exactly what he doesn't do? Yes, that too.

I belong to several men's groups. I've been attending them for years now. I've sat around the proverbial campfire and listened much more than I have spoken. I've heard men share stories about raising their sons and daughters, their victories, graduations and births, and their defeats, failures, addictions and deaths. All of the stories taken together give me strength that I can be a father to little Jack no matter what his life journey may look like.

I didn't always feel this way. I was scared to be a grownup, scared to be a husband, scared to be a father. I wasn't scared like seeing a tiger in an open field. It was less focused fear, more like a persistent worry underneath my daily living. Somehow I wasn't going to make it. Now Jack is here and I have those years of men's meetings in me, and I'm also thinking about all our ancestors in heaven looking out for him. Now I'm not so scared.

Our job is to keep Jack safe and clothed and loved. Our job is to get him to age eighteen with ten fingers and ten toes and an open, engaged and curious outlook on life. After eighteen, he is a grown-up in the eyes of the world. He makes his own choices. He dates. He works. He travels. He reads. Or he does none of those things. But the important thing is that he is running his own life. He is learning and living his path.

What if I could teach him that he's not alone through all of that? What if I could teach him that his Mommy and I, his grandparents here on earth and all his great grandparents up in heaven, that we all love him and are with him and are pulling for him? What if he walks into his life very clear about that? Would that be a contribution to him? Would he get the support and still understand that the choices are his to take? Yes. I declare he would.

Time will tell what it will be like for him. But for now, I can create how I choose to parent. I can choose the world I create for him.

My wife has blue eyes. I have brown. Little Jack has deep chocolate eyes. My dad has blue eyes and my mom has brown. My brother, sister and I all got mom's brown eyes. Charlie and my Texas cousins all have green or blue eyes, and I grew up thinking that it was better to have green or blue eyes.

I'm fast changing my opinion looking at my son. His skin is fair and his shiny chocolate eyes are all the more striking looking up at me. The linens of his crib are white and baby blue and sometimes when we put him in bed, his sleeping clothes are similar soft colors. In the dim light of morning his skin and his clothes and the crib all blend together, like pale, baby-colored camouflage.

But then he opens his eyes and I know exactly where he is. Those two solid spheres stare at me silently as he yawns and stretches and wonders when I'm going to change his diaper so he can go to Mommy and have breakfast. I'm in love with those eyes, those deep chocolate mirrors to his soul. He is looking up and I am looking down, with all my angel ancestors peering over my shoulder, and I know they are smiling.

The Christening — August 12, 2007

They're coming. This big Jersey family I've married into is on its way West for Jack's christening. Well, technically not everyone. It won't be as big as our Christmas gatherings, because Bonnie and Gary and their kids couldn't make it, nor Suzanne and David, Marisa's other siblings. But Grandma and Grandpa Szem are coming from South Carolina, and so are Marisa's brother Chris and his wife Lisa and their five kids from New Jersey, everyone getting on planes to Los Angeles. Uncle Jeff and Aunt Katherine, cousin Jay and his wife Kris and their son are all driving up from Orange County, no planes required. My mom and Travis are flying in from Dallas. My dad isn't coming, his distaste for plane trips post-9/11 unchanged; we got him to fly to Rhode Island for the wedding, and that was victory enough.

Marisa has ordered a cake, a big, professionally made cake with two flavors inside, chocolate cream on the left and strawberry shortcake on the right. I didn't know cakes could be so good. I'd tasted one just like it at the baby shower my UCLA colleagues threw for me, so for Jack's christening, we went to the same baker and ordered something similar.

Growing up Presbyterian, I'm used to calling this kind of event a baptism, not a christening. In our small congregation in Denison, there would only be a few baptisms a year, a single family with their new infant, and the baptism would be woven into the regular worship service. I remember my dad performing baptisms and they seemed noteworthy, something out of the usual worship routine. A special font held the baptismal water and the parents with their infant came and stood in the middle. A touch of water was applied to the baby and a few words spoken.

When we prepared for my own conversion to Catholicism earlier this year, we had to find out when I had been baptized. My preacher father had baptized me when I was an infant and I got to see the hand-written entry in Dad's ministerial journal, *November 30, 1969. Seven Months & Two Weeks. Made a face on the third sprinkling. Rather indignant!*

Mom looked through shoeboxes and came up with old photographs from my baptism, those three-inch square photos with the rounded corners from the 60s and 70s. In one photo, my skinny dad was standing at the pulpit holding his newly baptized son with my beautiful young mom standing next to him looking very peaceful. In a silly photo, taken afterwards, my dad is at the pulpit alone, with his hand raised and a big, pseudo-scary face suggesting he was practicing some fire and brimstone. Funny because I'd never seen a photo of my dad horsing around at work, funny too because we Presbyterians are very reserved and intellectual. In church, we don't genuflect when we enter a pew, or cross ourselves, or kneel during prayers. There's a seminary nickname for us, *the frozen chosen*, and before sobriety and Catholicism, that was a good description of me, living in my head, thinking all the time.

Now, being a converted Catholic in Los Angeles, I'm excited that we're going to have a christening. And it isn't going to be a small affair. St. Monica's, the church where we worship, is a Catholic community with thousands of members, and we will be christening a whole gaggle of new infants in one large, stand-alone service on a Sunday afternoon. We've had preparatory classes to learn about the spiritual gift being offered to our children, as well as hear logistics of when to arrive and where to park, always an important part of any gathering in LA.

Father Rohr's words from his CD are in my thoughts: *God doesn't love us because we are good, but rather God loves us because God is good. We don't earn God's love. It is a gift that is freely given and nothing we can do can either earn it or lose it.* That's one of the most beautiful sentiments I have ever heard. It is a north star to guide me as I try to be the kind of daddy I would hope to be. My job is to love my son. Guide him, yes. Parent him, yes. But love him no matter what. It's easy now that he's only an infant, but I know he will become a teenager and a young adult someday. My job is to love him through all of those chapters unconditionally, the way I'm learning to appreciate that God loves all the people on this planet, no one left out.

Our christening weekend proceeds at great pace, with the grand event to happen on Sunday. Saturday morning is brunch in the backyard at our home. Lots of eager pre-teen and teenage Jersey cousins are wide-eyed at the Hollywood possibilities on tap for the day. After brunch, everyone disperses for their various activities, and we have a few quiet hours before reassembling for an afternoon cookout in the backyard with both family and our neighbors.

My brother-in-law Chris is Marisa's oldest sibling. He and his wife Lisa had three children and assumed their baby-making was complete when along came their final pregnancy which turned out to be twins—Amanda and Brianna! Wow, from three to five children. I'm amazed just imagining raising five kids. I have to watch my mind as it starts comparing me to Chris and determining that I don't measure up. *Chris didn't raise one child, he's raised five. What's the matter with you Dylan? Loser...* As ever, my mind is not my friend.

Chris and Marisa quickly determine the one flaw in our cookout plan is that we don't have a grill. It's about 4:30 in the afternoon when Chris, having taken the matter into his own hands, pulls up in the large SUV he's rented to people-move his brood and from the back pulls out a brand new Weber grill that we assemble and use. Again, my mind goes off with endless comparisons: *He flew seven people cross country. He rented a big SUV, not the tin-can-tiny compact you always rent. He didn't pitch in with a bucket of chicken like you'd bring, but rather brought steaks AND a grill. Dylan, what kind of loser are you...*

At moments like these I'm grateful, so grateful, for the lessons I've learned in sobriety. There's an adage of *don't compare my insides to other people's outsides,* and the wisdom of it comes to me. Chris is living his life as best he's able, but I don't know what it's like to be him. He may have his own struggles that he has to deal with. Another idea I've learned is to *be of service,* instead of naval-gazing, move some furniture, grab a screwdriver and assemble a grill and get some steaks cooking. Father Rohr's observation that Catholicism is an earthy, hands-on, eating, drinking and celebrating faith becomes real to me when I see my new, extended family come together for these celebrations.

The christening on Sunday went well. We had a special outfit for Jackson to wear, a white contraption with snaps in all different places. We waited our turn in the sanctuary with our family all around us. When it was our turn, and the waters washed over our infant son, I was grateful. I *get* to be part of this big Polish-Jersey clan, I get to be sober and I get to be Catholic. I'm grateful to be raising our son surrounded by a village.

Shoulder to Shoulder — August 28, 2007

We went to see the doctor today for Jack's four month check up. Four months and two days, to be exact. He is 27 ½ inches long and 17 pounds, 6 ½ ounces. Later I realized we weighed him with a wet diaper. So we took the diaper off, weighed it alone, and subtracted 6 ounces.

Jack's a big baby for his age. Today the nurse told us he was in the 92nd percentile for weight and the 95th percentile for length. At lunch, someone guessed he was 9 months old. Both his grandfathers are over six feet tall. He gets his height from them, his red hair from Barbara and his chocolate eyes from Ginny. Everyone added something to baby Jack.

"Four months? Really? Wow! He's a big guy!"

His body is big and his head is big, too. Our pediatrician, Dr. Sloninsky, noticed his hat size at the two month check up. She watched it at the three month checkup and again, today, at four.

"Let's get him an ultrasound," she said, her tone steady and light. "His head has grown another two centimeters this month. While there's still an opening in his skull bones, we can make an ultrasound, no radiation, and get a look at how he's doing."

Dr. Sloninsky is our second pediatrician. Marisa fired our first one, who came highly recommended, but, similar to the doctors in the hospital, she was very green. Her bedside manner wasn't that great, and she hadn't yet figured out how to run her office. The nurses were calling the shots and the whole place felt chaotic.

An early experience was a warning signal. At one month, Jack was having white stuff on his tongue. We went to see our young pediatrician to find out what it was. She told us to go home and try to wipe it off with a cloth. If it came off, it was just breast milk, but if not, it was probably a condition called thrush. We were exhausted that day. But we went home and followed directions, and somewhere in the middle of wrestling Jack, trying to wipe his tongue, Marisa decided we needed a more attentive pediatrician. What were we doing trying to diagnose our son? Wasn't that why she went to medical school? We had been so spoiled by Dr. Kerr that wrestling to wipe a tongue and self-diagnose seemed like the wrong thing to do.

Marisa fired that first pediatrician and started looking for a replacement. Dr. Sloninsky turns out to be Dr. Kerr's personal pediatrician, which is how Marisa found her. Dr. Sloninsky is from Argentina, but she married a Polish man and took his non-Spanish sounding name. Since Marisa's name was Szemplenski growing up, we felt encouraged by the Polish connection.

When we met her, Dr. Sloninsky's first words to Jack, uttered in her lilting Spanish accent, were, "Oh, he is perfect, a perfect baby. Look at this big perfect baby."

Sold. Done. She had us at *hola*.

Marisa made the return visit to the hospital for Jack's ultrasound later that afternoon. After the technician performed the procedure, Marisa had to wait for the results. I had gone with her for the first visit in the morning, but I couldn't take off the afternoon, so had to hear about everything over the phone.

And what I was hearing on the phone, I didn't like one bit. Marisa was waiting for a long time. What if they screwed up? What if they found bad news? He's a big kid. He's got a big head. Big deal. This sucks. Leave him alone.

Dr. Sloninsky was reassured by the results of the ultrasound but not satisfied. "We don't know yet," she told Marisa tentatively. "There's a little bit of extra fluid in his head. There's no encephalitis, but we're going to have to get an expert opinion from a doctor who is on vacation right now. Typically, he will want to do an MRI."

An MRI? What the hell? What about the radiation? That doesn't sound good, I thought to myself as Marisa related these details. *Take a breath. This will all work out. This is just a precaution,* I told myself, but my mind was sneering at me the entire drive home. *Jack's gonna die. Jack's gonna die,* my mind chanted, poking at me with the sharp stick of my worst fear.

I called recovery friends. I called my parents. I was hoping to deflate my anxiety and arrive home calm. Marisa was focused on Jack. She had spent the whole day with him in a hospital. She didn't need to take care of me, too. It helps our marriage for me to have support from other people.

Marisa needed a break when I got home. I took Jack—my very much alive and happy son—outside. We lay down on a blanket under a tree in the yard. I got flat on my back next to him and looked up, so we were seeing the same view. The long, willow-like branches of the Chinese elm swayed in the evening air. Lying flat and looking up was like looking at a gigantic aquarium with water plants drifting in slow motion. I could see why Jack becomes so calm when we take him outside and he looks up at the trees. There is so much to see in a tree. He can be very upset, but if we take him where there are trees to watch, it almost always calms him down.

We lay there, shoulder to shoulder. He was looking at the swaying branches, his eyes peering in an upwards direction, patiently taking everything in. He was cooing and smiling and happy. I was on the blanket, just like him. We were side by side, each on our backs, looking up. I looked over at my son. He looked over at me. His expression said, "See. Isn't this cool Daddy? You don't need to worry. Everything is going to be fine."

For me, it was the best moment of our life together, so far. We were connected. My fears fell back and my mind shut up. The tension in my shoulders eased and I slowed my breathing. For that moment, everything was fine. It was the highlight of the Jack journey, and so I wrote a poem to commemorate the moment.

On the Blanket

With my son looking up,

At trees looking down.

Our eyes meet,

We are one.

It's gonna be okay, Daddy.

MRI — August 19, 2007

Humm… Okay, so we are going to have an MRI performed on our little Jackson this Friday. He can only eat once in the 12 hours before the procedure. Only once? He's going to be cranky. I'm able to leave work early on that Friday before Labor Day Weekend. That's good. Our son will have anesthesia and an MRI. That's bad.

Today, we talked to Marisa's cousin Jay who is a doctor. He has a buddy who is a brain doctor. Her cousin will consult with his buddy tomorrow, and we'll call back afterwards and hopefully get some reassurance. How lucky is that, to have a doctor in the family? Marisa's nursing Jack for the final time tonight. We'll put him down to sleep, and that will complete his day.

So. Our little son is going to have a procedure. That is all. He will have an MRI and then we will know more than we know now.

I met with my recovery group for lunch today, and talked with a man whose child has had multiple surgeries. Because they both have busy careers, he and his wife have a deal with their child. Mommy is there when the anesthesia is given. Then Daddy is always there when it's time to wake up after the surgery. It humbled me to hear what he goes through in his journey as a parent.

I have another dear friend in recovery who lost a 16-year-old son. He had somehow managed to work through his grief and counseled me about little

Jack. *"Don't put him in the cancer ward just because he needs one little test,"* he said. My mind, of course, had a cancer ward or worse already picked out. My mind, I've learned as a parent, is not my friend. In fact, it's usually the direct opposite of a friend, pumping me full of doom and gloom at every unexpected event.

Marisa put Jack in his crib and brought me a bowl of ice cream, some freaky flavor with swirls and chunks and other stuff in it. Why is it that all desserts have to overlap? Whatever happened to *just* chocolate, to *just* vanilla? Or to separate categories, like candy *or* ice cream? It's all just one enormous, sweet, blended, dessert-burrito today.

And speaking of worries. Next week my wife goes back to work. Her maternity leave ends the day that we get our MRI, the Friday before Labor Day Weekend. We have used up all her maternity leave, all her sick leave, all her vacation—all of it. On Tuesday, we'll have our first day of in-home babysitters, or *nannies*, as they say here in Los Angeles.

After all our interviews, we chose two caregivers, one who will come in the morning and a second who will come in the afternoon. We can't afford to have them for the full work day, so we're going to stagger our work time hours. Marisa will go to work early and get home by 5:00 p.m. I will start work late and come home late. This means we will *only* have to pay for childcare from 9 to 5, for eight hours a day. At $15 an hour, that will *only* be $600 a week, or *only* $2400 a month. We cannot afford this. We are going to have to borrow from our savings to make ends meet.

And I'm still not comfortable about it. Are they trustworthy? Will they take good care of our precious Jack? What would we do if they didn't? Do we pay their taxes? How do would we even do that? Who cares for *their* kids while they are caring for our kid? This is one more chapter in the whole experience of being a parent. It is one more *AFGO*, as we would say in recovery. *A*nother *F*lippin' *G*rowth *O*pportunity.

That's what I get from recovery meetings, made-up words like *AFGO* and the humor that goes with them. I can bring the biggest, most crushing problem to a meeting, and if I listen to what others are sharing, I'll hear bigger, badder problems than mine. And there will be humor. A few weeks after 9/11, when it was looking like my whole team at Siemens was about to be laid off, I talked about my apprehension in a 7:00 a.m. morning meeting. "Bring a box!" came a reply from one person, "so you can take home all the stuff in your desk at work, if you do get laid off." I came into the meeting thinking it was the end of the world, and I left laughing with people who were telling me to bring a box and enjoy my *AFGO*, supporting me with smiles on their faces, love in their hearts, and pats on the back. It is a great way to go through life, having such a community around me.

Hmmm... So what will we do while we wait for modern medicine to give us more information? Last year, modern medicine told us we couldn't get pregnant. Thank God we listened to old fashioned Chinese medicine. Old fashioned Chinese medicine gave us different instructions to follow, assuring us by saying, "Wait. Your baby come any day now."

Our son's body is big compared to other babies. He is a big baby and he has a big head. To me, that is pretty straight forward. Big baby, big head. Wouldn't we be more worried if he had a little head? Our cousin Jay got back to us and said, "It sounds like a soft call. Meaning that there is not a lot of danger, and they are just double-checking to make sure all is well."

✳✳✳✳✳✳✳✳

It's Saturday morning of Labor Day weekend. Marisa's feeding Jack. I'm in the kitchen with coffee brewing. Yesterday, we had an MRI performed on Jack. We went to Cedars-Sinai in Los Angeles, where all the movie stars go to die—or have their babies. Everyone was professional and competent. We think insurance will pay for most of it, but even 20% of a procedure like that may screw up our budget. Baby medicine is so fun. You spin the wheel and wonder how much things will cost, and the bills float in months after each procedure.

So, we got an MRI, a fancy photo of our son's brain.

Jack is big. He's been a 95th + percentile baby in height and weight each time we've gone in for his monthly pediatric visit. That means that he is tall and heavy compared with some group of babies that they've measured in the past. I always wonder who those babies are. Does it include little babies in Mexico? Does it include tall babies from Scandinavia? Does it include corn-fed babies from Iowa?

At Jack's two month checkup, our doctor noted that his head circumference was big too. Almost at the borderline of how much it should be. "We'll want to watch that," she'd said. She measured his head at the three month visit. She measured his head at the four month visit. We needed an ultrasound. We got that, and it confirmed there was fluid, but it was inconclusive. So we came for the MRI on Friday.

To even schedule the MRI so soon was a tribute to my wife who worked the phones and got us an appointment. I took the day off work. Our original afternoon appointment got bumped to the morning.

We arrived at 9:30 a.m. at Cedars Sinai. Nice people greeted us. Our nurse explained how things would go. One of us would go in with him for the procedure. It would take about an hour. Later, our actual doctor came out. He explained things again. He was the doctor who would manage the MRI and take the images, but not the doctor who would interpret the results. He asked us not to get our expectations too high about hearing results today.

He took us back into the MRI area. "Now give him a kiss and we take him from here," the doctor told us. *Wait, I thought the nurse said one of us was going back, too?* Apparently not. Marisa and I sat together in the lobby. We held hands and said a prayer. We read magazines. Thirty minutes passed. One hour passed. Ninety minutes passed. The nurse said an hour, but it was taking longer. Where was our baby? Dark images crashed from the background of my mind. There must be a problem…

Finally, at an hour and forty five minutes, they came to get us. We went back behind the big doors again and there was our little son Jack. He was wrapped in a white blanket, but he was placed in the middle of an adult gurney and looked tiny and helpless. He had the oxygen mask over his face, and there was an indicator light on his big toe. His tiny chest was covered with circle patches with wires coming out of them. His right wrist was wrapped in gauze and taped, and there was an IV connected to his hand with a needle.

And he was crying. Softly. Slowly. He was crying and it was not his normal voice. That was a scary thing to hear. This cry was unnatural. He was still coming off the anesthesia. It was weak and helpless sounding. His tiny body was dwarfed by all the machines.

The extra delay was because they didn't have a receiving bed for him, but no one had come to tell us that. Now there was a bed free and we made our winding way through hallways, up elevators, through a baby unit where a stern nurse lectured the man leading us, saying, "You shouldn't have come through here." We entered the PACU, post anesthesia care unit. We were the only baby in the unit, and we got a crib at the back that was multiple primary colors. Jack was crying more normally now. Loud and interruptive—I am Jack and hear me roar. There were lots of elderly patients in the ward. I did the daddy thing and stared at my son instead of making eye contact with annoyed people.

Marisa fed him. We serendipitously saw a doctor who is also an Executive MBA student in our program at UCLA. He works in this part of the hospital, and he was like an angel. He spent ten minutes with us, giving us a bonus consult and much needed reassurance.

They let us go after an hour. We paid for parking and went home. We got In-N-Out hamburgers for lunch on the way. We took a big nap after our late lunch. We wouldn't know the results until after the weekend.

It had been a big day. Jack was back and for now, that was very good. A month before at Sears, we took pictures of his *outsides*, which had looked perfect. Today we took pictures of his *insides*, and I am praying that they will be perfect, too.

Results — October 14, 2007

It's been six weeks since I last wrote. I've tried to distract myself, but I've been worried. Worried about Marisa's maternity leave ending. Worried about Jack home without us during the day since the nannies have started coming. Worried about my job. I've worried like I was getting paid for it. But for now at least, I have not been worried about Jack's big hat size.

On Tuesday, September 4, the day after Labor Day weekend, we went to see the MRI expert. He looked at the results and told us they were okay. *Benign external hydrocephalous.* Three big words that meant there was a little bit of extra fluid, but it wasn't doing anything and it should get better. Especially since there weren't any other symptoms showing up, the doctor said he felt good about it and that we should come back for a follow up. Six weeks later, we had the follow up with the same expert, and he was pleased with what he saw in Jack. He said we didn't need to see him again, that our regular pediatrician, Dr. Sloninsky, would be able to take it from here.

Being a dad is awesome and being a dad is humbling. I can't predict nor prevent a medical situation. How do parents deal with ill children? My heart and compassion are so expanded in the five months I've been a father. I've spent a lot of time thinking about how I would respond if Jack was not healthy, if he had a chronic problem. I've always been scared that I would not have enough character to deal with a real challenge, a terminal illness or some big disaster.

I have thought about how much harder it must have been to raise kids in the past. I have thought about my ancestors, about old movies of tough times on the prairie or in some war, parents trying to raise their kids while their world was falling apart. My professor in graduate school said that 150 years ago, birth certificates weren't even processed until a few weeks after birth because infant mortality was so high it was better to see if the child actually lived before bothering with the paperwork. What would that be like?

And I have thought about my family and friends in the here and now. I didn't realize how many people were praying for us and pulling for us when Jack had his MRI. One of my mom's Presbyterian church-lady friends, a woman well into her 80s, took on being the prayer leader and made special efforts to let my mom know how many people had her grandson in their thoughts. How many Catholic candles did Jack's grandma Barbara light for him these last two months?

All of this worrying has had me think about what I am doing in my life. I have been wondering if my contribution in life might be to stand up and speak. Maybe. On *60 Minutes* tonight, I watched a report on a mega-preacher. Seven million people listen to him every week. The critics say he only talks about the good half of the Bible. That he leaves out suffering, sin, and the tougher parts of following a spiritual path. *God's nice. You're nice. Be nice.* That was how one critic summarized the mega-preacher's message. I realized this is the same preacher, Joel Osteen, whom I had heard on TV back at Christmas while I was working out on the treadmill.

My question to the critic is, "Was that comment very nice?"

My second question to the critic is, "Does the preaching make a difference? Does it lead to results in people's lives?" Because if it does—and the huge audiences that listen would testify to this effect—then what is the problem? The one day I'd ever heard him preach, over the TV and in an empty hotel workout room, he'd made a difference for me.

And here we are, six weeks past Marisa's maternity leave. She has gone back to work and we have had six weeks of in-home babysitting. We are starting to get a rhythm with our two babysitters. Marisa leaves for work at 7:00 a.m. I hang out with Jack until the first caregiver arrives at 9:00 a.m., when I leave for my job. In the middle of the day, while Marisa and I are both away, the second caregiver comes and relieves the first woman. It would be simpler to have one person the whole day, but we couldn't find anyone whose schedule was free for the whole day. Marisa gets home by 5:00 p.m., and the second nanny goes. I get home about 7:30 in the evening. Jack hangs out through all of it.

Marisa is so much calmer than me. I think because she has spent her whole career working in hotels and hired so many people, she is used to managing and delegating, which is exactly what we are doing.

I watched my mom and dad raise their three kids very differently than we are raising Jack, and I don't have much comfort in all of this. I still get thoughts during the day about what would happen if something went wrong. The thoughts are always bad. They are always a worst case scenario.

The actual results, however, don't match the bad thoughts. Jack is happy and healthy every evening when I get home. Marisa is always with him since she is the first one home, and he is always doing great. Marisa stopped nursing him directly a month ago when his first teeth arrived right after four months. She's using the breast pump, and her goal is to raise him on breast milk until he is one year old.

He is still a big boy, over 19 pounds now, coming up on six months. I have no control over his health, his daycare, our finances, but the results, so far, are okay. He is thriving and is happy. Marisa is happy. That is enough for now, and if I can just stay focused on those results, grateful for what's really going on, things aren't really so bad.

What a Smile — November 18, 2007

Hi Little Jack,

You're not so little anymore. At seven months, you're over 20 pounds now, at least 30 inches long, but you wiggle so much, we can't measure you exactly. I'm sorry I haven't written much in September, October and November. You got us a little worried for awhile, and I got busy with work as a distraction.

Tonight, as I sat here I remembered a smile you beamed at me today. It was so joyful and pure. It gave me encouragement to write to you tonight. You're asleep in the other room. Your mom's already gone to bed, too.

You're changing so much. This past week, your babysitters taught you to clap when they say *Bravo*. I've seen you do it, sort of. Your arms move and you seem to know what's happening. I saw your smile change this week. It's a much wider smile now. And you are so generous with it. You light up for me, for Mommy, for your babysitters. You smile for new people if we speak to you in soft, easy tones. You're a beacon of happiness.

I think I stopped writing because I don't have anything close to the words to describe how wonderful it is to be your father. The more I write, especially on this topic of being your father, the more I feel like a fraud. You are healthy. You are happy. You are the most beautiful baby I've ever seen. How can I write about that? You're a gift from God. I didn't do anything except gratefully receive you.

An aside. This week your mom told me that there was a surprise for me on the answering machine. I found a message from Dr. Mary Kerr. It was directed to me specifically, saying thank you for the letter I wrote to her, thanking her for delivering you and taking care of Mommy back on April 25th. She said it was the best letter she'd ever gotten. She said she takes it out and reads it when she's having a bad day. That's you, Jack. That's the inspiration you are to me and others.

So about this smile you have. A lot of times you don't look at me. You're in a calm, looking-around mode, and you seem to look anywhere but directly at me. Then, there are those other times. Your eyes dance around. They find my eyes. They stop and lock and *BOOM*, that smile erupts across your face. Jack, it is an incredible feeling to be on the receiving end of that smile. It's overwhelming.

Your wonderful mommy was talking to me at dinner tonight. She was telling me how much she loves our life. She said that if the whole world disappeared and it was just us three, that she'd be okay with that. That's how much she appreciates you and me and us.

You have another new smile that's shown up recently. You'll be sitting up and looking around and then you'll get happy. Your hands will grab at your legs or push flat on the floor. You'll shrug your shoulders and peer about and BEAM again. I can't get enough of it.

Then there's a third smile, when you are standing in your new orange walker that Mommy got for you last week. You're in the middle of that donut-looking device and you're playing with all the different attachments and you're teetering left and right and when you look up your face is happy all the way across.

Jack, you are a joy. You are the joy of our life. Your mommy and I are so overwhelmed by having you join us. You are a gift and we are so grateful to have you with us.

I can't wait for Christmas this year. You're so big and strong now. It's much more fun to hold you now because I'm not worried anymore that you are too delicate. You hold your head up and you can sit up (most of the time, except when you forget and teeter over), and it is fun being with you.

You know what else we did today for the first time? I raised you over my head and put you on my shoulders. I did it while Mommy was at the grocery store, getting all our food for Thanksgiving week. You and I were in the living room, and we could see ourselves in the big mirror over the fireplace. You kept grabbing my hair in your hands and seeing yourself in the mirror and smiling and laughing. I was bouncing on my toes and swaying left and right. You were riding up there, looking about and having a blast.

Last night, Saturday night, we took you to church for the 5:30 service. Your mommy was content to stand at the back so that is what we did. We were behind the back glass wall, looking into the sanctuary and listening to the service. I'd had you with me all day Saturday, from 10 a.m. until we met Mommy for dinner. You'd gone with me to a recovery meeting, and a friend of mine spoke in the group to say how much he appreciated seeing me with you in the back of the meeting.

Then you went with me to work, where we hung out in my office from 12 to 4, while Daddy completed the draft of his 2007 performance evaluation. Then on the way home, we called Mommy and decided we should meet for dinner and then try church if your energy permitted. You did great at dinner, so we made our way to church. There you were in the back, behind the glass wall, and you were happy there, too. There was an Asian family with a 13-month-old son, and you and he made eye contact through the glass and smiled at each other.

When it was time for the Eucharist, I proudly carried you as Mommy and I walked down the center of the church, which we do each time. There was a silent moment in the prayer, as we stood in the middle of the congregation, and you let out a wonderful shriek that filled up the entire stone room, pure, vibrant, delicious joy.

It's so good to put words down. It's so good to be your father and have these moments and to share them with the future you. Thank you for coming into our life. I love your mommy more than anything. She wanted you so badly. You mean so much to her. You mean so much to me. Thank you for being our son.

Love you Jack,

Your Poppa

Adjustable Rate — November 26, 2007

We bought our home three years ago, in 2004, using one of those financial devices that would come to be seen as the Tasmanian Devils of the economic landscape, an adjustable rate mortgage (ARM). Before, we lived in a third floor apartment in Santa Monica facing west and three blocks from the beach. On windy afternoons, if you stood on our balcony and waited for the trees to part, you could see a tiny sliver of the Pacific Ocean far in the distance.

Walking the affluent streets of Santa Monica and dreaming when we saw homes for sale, we soon learned that every price tag had a *point* in it, as in one *point* six million dollars or two *point* three million dollars. We were not *point people* even before our wedding depleted our bank accounts, and yet we watched the papers and started dreaming about finding a home of our own.

Our friend Natalie, in addition to being one of the three people on the planet we let babysit Jack, also worked in the loan origination business down in Orange County, and she began talking to Marisa about how we could get ourselves into a home using an ARM.

"It's not the way our parents' generation did it with that 20% down that is so hard to swing, based on the prices of homes in Los Angeles." She informed us, with her gleaming elf-like smile.

I had a Saturday workday with my part-time MBA students and I returned to our apartment and the delicious aroma of steaks cooking over an open flame. Natalie and Marisa had prepared a feast. We ate and they listened to my UCLA experiences recruiting new MBA students that day. We had our new #1 ranking, which was fun to brag about to prospective students. When I had run out of things to say there was a pause and then Marisa said, "Dylan, I think that Natalie and I found our new home. It's in Culver City and we can go check it out tonight after dinner if you're game."

I was feeling so happy with my steak meal that I couldn't say no and after dinner we drove the few miles over to a quaint, tree-lined neighborhood, like Mayberry in the 1950s. The sun was setting as we pulled up to a white picket fence surrounding a single-storied white home with green trim. There was a curving sidewalk leading up to the door and in the front yard stood a magnificent tree whose branches made a canopy that was lit from underneath by the glow of the old-fashioned, post-style street lamp on the corner.

The moment was one of those perfect California slices of time that somehow make it worth all the hassle living out here. As I looked at the flower beds full of impatiens and walked up to the door a thought blazed through my mind, "Please don't tell me we can't afford this."

We met the realtor and walked through the echoing rooms on beautiful hardwood floors. The home was built in 1939 and had the very same smell of plaster walls I remembered from childhood visits to Harold Dear and Bobby Dear's home in Dallas.

The actual answer may technically have been that we couldn't afford it, but this is California, a state both envied and ridiculed for its exasperating optimism and we strong armed our way into owning a piece of the golden state. Not only did we not have 20%, we didn't even have the 2% that they asked for as earnest money. Marisa's older brother Chris and my friend Wendy each loaned us 1% to afford the earnest money which we then repaid to them after we closed escrow. With no money down we had secured a safe, small magnificent home in west Los Angeles.

I of course, additionally secured for myself one more massive worry to add to my insatiable appetite for *what could go wrong*. My worry planning our wedding, my worry that hovered over both of our pregnancies, that same type of worry muscle was flexing with glee in the face of two mortgages, a bi-annual property tax bill and insurance payments, all on Marisa's junior executive pay and my blazing contribution as a state employee working in education. "We'll never make it," screamed out my doomsday-predicting mind. Marisa didn't miss a beat and had never seemed happier as we moved into our new home. When she has voices in her head, she goes all Jersey on them and tells them to take a seat.

So here we were in the fall of 2007, and the time to re-finance had arrived. Once more all the calls to banks and loaning agencies, once more all the mumbo-jumbo jargon of home loans, and once more into another ARM, this one for a longer period of time but an ARM nonetheless. My brain was quick with the comparisons, "My dad never put himself into an ARM. I bet Brady and Jeff can afford 30 year fixed rate mortgages. What's wrong with me?"

We keep working. We keep praying. We parent our little son each and every day. My mentor in recovery asks me, "What is the worst that will happen? You can't afford it, so you move into an apartment. Do you really think God is going to dump you on your head?"

Why yes, that is exactly what my mind thinks, me of little faith.

One of my many character defects is impatience, one of my biggest actually. I want what I want when I want it. But being an adult doesn't work that way. I'm building muscle to keep going even when I don't know the outcome, to take small steps even when the goal seems too big or too far in the future. I've learned to practice staying sober one day at a time and I've extended that practice to being faithful to Marisa, to being an employee, to being a homeowner, to being a father, all one day at a time. Give us *this* day our daily bread. It's right there in the Lord's Prayer. When I can focus on my *daily* bread, not my future bread, I find that my plate is always full. There is nourishment enough for today.

Cemetery Sudoku — January 15, 2008

My plane landed in Phoenix early, close to rush hour. Taxi and rental car both cost the same amount, but a rental car would allow me to visit my maternal grandparents before I had to give a recruitment speech for my job that evening at a local hotel. At the airport, I followed the signs and shuttles and placed a phone call to reserve a rental car. I spent the extra $10 of my own money and got the GPS unit. I called my mother, got the name and address of the cemetery where my grandparents were buried, and dialed it into the little dashboard navigator.

"Oh, and by the way, when you get there, it's easy to find their gravesite. It's under an olive tree, where the graveled area meets the grassy area," Mom told me.

My mom grew up in Tempe, Arizona. In the 1950s, before urban sprawl hit, Tempe was still out in the country. To go on a date with my mom or one of her two sisters, a guy had to drive out of town some ways and then down the long driveway that was the entrance to my grandfather's small homestead and ranch.

In the 1970s, when I was a kid visiting my grandparents with my family, Tempe still smelled overwhelmingly of orange blossoms, depending on the season. The ranch was closer to town by then, Tempe having grown, and a big highway spur, Highway 60—the "Superstition"—had grown up along one side of the ranch and interrupted the sun-up to sun-down horizon that my mom grew up with. But my grandparents' ranch was still a paradise to visit. There was a modest, two-story farm house with everything impressive to a young boy surrounding it: horses, chickens, dogs and cats, and flocks of guard geese who hissed like hellions. These my grandfather had bought to eat the weeds in the orange orchard that covered the back half of the world he had created. My grandmother had a small building that she converted into a library. It seemed normal to me as a child, but looking back I'm more impressed. A *library*? She had a fully stocked library in her house

I was remembering snippets of those 1970s visits as I followed the sing-songy, lady GPS voice towards the cemetery. "Turn left in 500 yards... 300 yards..."

Texas to Arizona by car in the 1970s, when my dad was a small town minister and our family car was a 1969 VW bus, was a big trip, both financially and distance-wise. I think we must have averaged a trip every other year, making the long exit from Dallas to El Paso to cut the corner of New Mexico and finally come into the "Valley of the Sun" of Phoenix. We did it often enough to make memories. Now that I have my own son, I see with new eyes the goal of making memories.

"Arriving at destination," my GPS lady-friend announces. I keep waiting for the GPS people to install a sexy voice option, "Grocery store ahead...big fella." I waited to cut through the thickening afternoon traffic. A hole opened up, and I darted my rental car into the quiet of a desert cemetery.

I tried to think back to my last visit. I couldn't actually remember the visit itself. Rather, I remembered two images, one a video I'd made in the cemetery with my grandmother the last time she and I had visited Grandpa's grave together, and the second image a still photograph of my tall cousin Joel leaning against the olive tree by Grandmother's gravesite on the day of her burial.

It was the olive tree memory of Joel that guided me as I got out of my car, looking to find their headstone, Grandma and Grandpa. The cemetery was larger than I remembered. Most childhood places revisited get smaller. It was funny that this wasn't the case today. There were also more olive trees. A lot more.

No one else was around. No cars. No people. The traffic and the freeway weren't that far away, but here in the actual cemetery they both faded into the distance. I saw a big desert jackrabbit up ahead, the kind with the long lope and the black accents at the end of their ears. That took me back to the 70s again. Jackrabbits and road runners were two of the more exotic animals we'd see, my younger brother Jon and me, as we prowled around Grandpa's ranch. Rabbits in Arizona were different in size and coloring, and road runners didn't even exist where our family lived in Texas.

I tested a few olive trees, remembering the photo and also watching for where "the grass meets the gravel." This wouldn't take too long, I thought. But I didn't have any luck. I dialed up my mom again.

"I'm here in the cemetery. It's a calm January afternoon. It must be in the 60s and the buttes are red and orange and beautiful," I reported.

Even though my mom left Arizona at 18 and lived the rest of her life in Texas, a part of her always feels connected to the southwest. She'd been driving the first time we spoke, and now she was back home, so I was hoping this second conversation would yield more clues. She repeated her directions but didn't have any new details. Instead, she suggested I call her brother or her sisters, my uncle and aunts. I reached one aunt. No luck on gravesite details, but a nice conversation.

After that I reached cousin Joel, the same cousin in my memory of the olive tree. Joel is one of my favorite cousins and we caught up on jobs, kids and life. He didn't know where the gravesite was either, but we were having a great conversation. Not knowing what else to do, I went back to the edge of the cemetery and started over. I methodically marched up and down, looking for clues, the same way I work a Sudoku puzzle. Joel and I shared stories. He had a bum situation in a new job. I told him about my challenges last year with a promotion and then our pregnancy.

Up and down the cemetery row, slide over one row, repeat. I came across four other gravesites with my mother's maiden name, and finally, I found my grandparents' gravesite. There they were. There was the olive tree, which looked like all the other olive trees. My rental car was small and distant across the way. My dress shoes had a layer of mauve dust on them from crunching along the gravel. The afternoon had grown longer.

Joel and I completed our conversation, and I put my cell phone on vibrate. I didn't know what else to do, so I knelt down by their graveside and I said the Lord's Prayer. Then, I told Grandma and Grandpa about their great-grandson, Jack. I let them know he was healthy and happy, that he was a redhead with a ready smile. I thanked Grandma again for being a librarian and an avid reader, and for supporting my imagination when as a sixth grader, I received from her my very own Dungeons and Dragons starter kit. I was the first boy in my circle to know about D&D. Lots of teenage boys play D&D, but how many were introduced to it by their grandmothers? Some of my friends' parents heard D&D was somehow devilish, but I remember thinking, *How could it be bad? I got it from Grandma!*

Kneeling at her grave, I told her that we were reading lots of books to Jack, every night before sleepy time. I know that I get much of my love of language from her. I told them I was blissfully happy in my marriage.

I plucked an orange from an orange tree nearby, remembering how big Grandpa's orange orchard had seemed when I was a kid, how scary his guard geese had been. I remembered a visit to this same cemetery with my grandmother when she was still alive. "Those are sour oranges," she had said. "You can't eat them."

The white noise of the traffic seemed even farther away. It was quiet in the deep, deserted pocket of the afternoon in this cemetery. I was aware of my ancestors and of all the lives of all the people buried here. I felt small and I felt peaceful.

I placed my orange—my sour orange—on top of Grandma and Grandpa's gravestone. It felt fitting to honor them with the fruit, even if it wasn't sweet and edible. Their great grandson was alive and well in the world, and I wanted to acknowledge them for that precious gift. I looked up to the heavens and I smiled, before walking back across the gravel path to my rental car.

We Are All Of Us Connected — February 21, 2008

Our nanny told us Thursday afternoon that Jack was coming down with something. Her daughter had a stomach bug earlier in the week, and Jack's symptoms appeared similar—weak appetite and lethargic. Jack slept poorly Thursday night, and by Friday morning, we knew he had the bug, too. Our two nannies, the AM and the PM team respectively, were cancelled for the day. Maybe Jack got the stomach bug from one of them, but regardless, we didn't want him giving it to anyone else.

Marisa called in sick to her job to take care of him. We agreed that I would take him Saturday and give her a few hours at the office to make up some of the time she'd lose staying home Friday.

The plan was working as well as could be hoped. Jack's energy was up and down. He'd wake up and seem okay at first, only to poop out soon after. He had a low grade fever and he wasn't eating too much. Marisa kept him drinking liquids and making sure he stayed warm.

We all three had breakfast morning Saturday together, and then Marisa left for a few hours while I entertained Jack for the middle part of the day. We didn't see ourselves attending Mass this weekend, so we resolved to a stay-home routine with the hopes of getting better by Monday.

But that didn't happen. The lag time must have been about 48 hours, because after two days of care giving, Marisa and I both woke up Sunday morning in the grips of the stomach bug. It was that deep, debilitating pain that only seems to come from the gut. It reminded me of bad hangover memories. Myself, I'm a chicken about pain and I can get stopped by a hangnail, but Marisa has a much higher pain tolerance. I knew things were bad when Jackson cried out from his room Sunday morning and she didn't want to get up to go check on him.

I pulled my aching body up and went to see that he was okay. Marisa lay in the bed. "How is he?" she asked quietly.

"He's crying, and I can't tell if he's any better," I reported, collapsing back on my side of the bed, breathless from the trip to the next bedroom.

We lay there for about 20 minutes while Jack cried half-heartedly from his crib.

"What are we going to do?" I finally asked, when it seemed that Marisa was stirring. We were still so early into parenting that we had a very small roster of babysitting options, only three people total, our moms and Natalie.

"I don't know. Natalie's in a class this weekend." Marisa said. "I'm not sure who we can call."

"I don't know about asking Victoria across the street," I replied. Victoria is our semi-retired neighbor who had volunteered to babysit, but we'd not yet taken her up on her offer. "I don't see her car in the driveway, and I would hate to get her sick from being around us," I said, half mumbling. "I don't know if I can even lift Jack out of his crib right now."

I went into the kitchen, warmed up a bottle of breast milk and brought it to Jack. He could have his breakfast and stay in his crib. He was fussing and crying, but the bottle got his attention and for some short minutes he seemed pacified.

After he finished his bottle, I hoisted his body out of the crib and rocked him very slowly in the rocking chair, trying to coax a burp while not making myself nauseous. A few minutes later, I heard the little release as an air bubble came up. He seemed revived, but I was exhausted from just sitting there with him in my arms.

At any moment, I expected Marisa to come in and take over, but the help never came. She was down even worse than I was, and so I limped around the entire morning feeling helpless and vulnerable. I couldn't get the nagging thought out of my mind: *What would happen if something happened, something serious, with both of us so completely incapacitated?* Being separated from family had never seemed as crucial as now. If we lived near either of our families, it would be just a phone call for help. But here, thousands of miles away in Los Angeles, with our one other babysitter Natalie not available, we felt isolated and alone. It was a long, slow Sunday.

We got better over the next couple days. The nannies came back and life resumed. My thoughts turned to parents who raise kids with chronic illnesses, and I wondered where they get their strength. I thought about single parents, trying to hold down jobs and keep families together. My Denison friend Steve became a single dad to his two sons when his wife and he divorced, and she gave him custody.

How does he do that?

It's such a joke to think we are ever "independent," able to rise kids and live our lives "on our own." More accurately, we are all of us connected—interdependent—so much more than we know.

We Won the Lottery — March 15, 2008

Jackson finally came off the waiting list and was offered a seat in the UCLA campus daycare center. It felt like we'd won the lottery.

We'd waited 18 months, making our deposit and putting his name on the waitlist back when Marisa was barely pregnant. The pecking order for seats starts with faculty at the top and then trickles down to administrators like me. At one point, I'd called to check and found we were #47 on the waiting list. Now, we were feeling lottery-lucky when we got a call saying a space was open for us if we wanted it.

We had three days to decide, but it didn't take that long. We said yes and were told Jack could start in two weeks. At almost 11 months, he'd be placed in the "Bunny Classroom" with the under one set. Our goal had been to keep him at home until he turned one, but we didn't have any control over when a seat opened up, so we decided to put him in a month early rather than lose the chance.

It was my job to tell Jack's two nannies that we wouldn't be needing their services any more. I was emotional about this, because I felt like I was firing them, when all they had done was provide excellent care over the last six months, consistent and loving. But upon hearing the news, they understood the change and seemed much calmer about it than I was. They both thought it would be good for Jack, that being around other kids would be a good change, and that they were running out of activities to keep him occupied for a whole day.

I felt a gratitude I couldn't express for the nannies' care of Jack, similar to my profound appreciation of Dr. Kerr and her care of Marisa and baby Jack in the hospital and beyond. I want to be there for my wife and son, but there are big, important things I can't do. My father delivered my sister Lisa in the backseat of a Volkswagen when he and mom ran out of gas on the way to the hospital, but there was no way I could have helped deliver Jack by C-section without Dr. Kerr. There was no way we could have cared for Jack and still managed our jobs without our two nannies these last six months. Raising a child takes so much from so many people.

The big day approached. There were papers to fill out for daycare, and Marisa and I each had to go to the doctor and have our own shots updated. We were given instructions for the diapers, bottles and ointments that we would supply in Jack's cubby at daycare. Then, on his first day, we both took a vacation day to be with him, per the recommended procedure. Before we entered the front doors, we took a picture of ourselves with Jack. I was feeling very proud, as if our son had just been admitted to the *real* UCLA!

My mom has a picture of me on my first day of Kindergarten. I'm standing in front of the chain-link fence with checkered pants and a red sweater with white diamond patterns on it. My hair was light blond and cut in the straight-bangs style of the mid-1970s. I was five years old on my first day of school, and now here we were with Jack, not even one year old on his first day.

As proud as I was, I was also feeling equally guilty, thinking that the way we were raising Jack wasn't as good as how my parents raised me, and that somehow, because he's going to daycare, I'm failing. I reminded myself that both nannies had told us the experience would be good for Jack. I remembered how we were lucky to come off the waitlist, that UCLA's center was top-notch, and that having Jack on-campus meant I would be close to him for drop-in visits when I could get away from my office. But still, the guilt lingered.

Jack's Bunny classroom was brand new, so a whole cohort of parents and children were beginning the daycare adventure together. I watched the other parents also adjusting to the first day of school. This was a big transition for everyone, and we all emptied our bags into our respective cubbies while exchanging smiles and hellos. Parents in their first year seem to be tired all the time, and we in the Bunny room were no exception.

The routine of the first day got underway. At nap time, the teachers encouraged parents to put down a nap pad and lie next to our child to sooth him or her to sleep. Jack was still on a two-naps-a-day schedule, and it took a while for him to fall asleep both morning and afternoon. Then it was time to have lunch, and while we'd remembered everything for Jack, we'd forgotten about lunch for ourselves. One of the other parents graciously shared an extra energy bar with us that we gobbled hungrily.

The first week was a transition week, and each day Jack stayed slightly longer at daycare. The goal was for him to be comfortable there a whole day by the second week. More or less, we stayed on schedule. The transition was equally as important for us parents as it was for the kids. Marisa and I needed to adjust to Jack's absence from our home and the fact that he was now going to be in a whole new world of people and playmates.

The new rhythm of daycare established itself over the next few months, with several benefits emerging that I hadn't anticipated. Immediately, I got five evenings a week back to spend with Marisa and Jack. We no longer had to stagger our workdays so that we would *only* pay for eight hours of childcare each day. Now that we were in daycare, we got to have a family dinner together again, which was a welcome gift.

It feels strange to leave work at 5:00 p.m., the time daycare is over, to go pick up Jack. In my 13 years of professional life, I've never left at 5:00, always staying an hour or two more to wrap up things, but the daycare center closes at 5:30 sharp, and there is a dollar-a-minute fine for being late. No one wants to be the delinquent parent, so the scene at the center turns into a Yuppie NASCAR event around 5:20 each afternoon with Prius and Volvo baby-movers parked cattywampus.

I still felt guilty leaving work so early, even though that is the time my workday technically ends. I even asked my boss about it, "Get out of here," he shot back. "You're a father now and you have responsibilities." It was great to get that support, but the nagging doubt never fully goes away.

Also welcome was the sense of community and "village" we got at the daycare center. Jack's teachers were calm and competent with both infants and parents, and suddenly we had a wealth of new people to ask questions of. It was educational to talk to the teachers and the other parents, and share ideas and experiences. I learned about other children's eating, sleeping and pooping habits. I also learned none of us was sleeping well at this stage.

The fear of Jack being absconded has left me entirely. As much as I appreciated the care Jack got at home in the six months prior, I could never shake the vague fear of our only born son being at home without us there. Especially on my more tired days, when I'd slept poorly and work seemed so busy, I would have moments of despair in my office, worrying that we would return to an empty house.

Our nannies, I need to emphasize, did *absolutely nothing* to earn my apprehension; quite the opposite, but I had the fear anyway. Maybe it was the contrast between my own small-town childhood with a stay-at-home mom, and this Los Angeles life with day-long nannies that was so foreign to me. Maybe there was no way I could have ever felt completely comfortable. My parents were always around when I was little, and in a small town, everyone knows everyone. Los Angeles is a very different world.

Another benefit was the daily drive to work with Jack in the back-seat. Since his daycare was closest to my job, I got to take him most days. I loved looking over my right shoulder and seeing him sitting in his car seat. I would talk to him and tell him about my day. As he got older, we went through different games. We spent several months spotting different colored buses, blue, orange, red and yellow. We would point out construction equipment after he turned two, and we started to let him watch *Bob the Builder* DVDs. The construction down the middle of the 405 was a rich stretch for us to find "scoops," "lofties" and "rollies," the names of the animated characters in Bob's building world.

For the first few months, I walked 15 minutes over a hill several times a week to have lunch with my son. I brought a sandwich while he ate his baby food. When he was 14 months, his nap times changed from two-a-day to one-a-day, and the single naptime landed often in the middle of the day, so our lunchtimes together soon stopped.

When he started, Jack was the oldest of the Bunnies by five or six months. After six weeks, he started pulling himself into a standing position along the baby furniture, and the program director decided he needed to be in a class with older kids. We did a transition to the Chicks Classroom where Jack became one of the youngest kids in a room of 12 other children, all age 12 to 24 months. We met new teachers, learned the new patterns, and started over. It seems that every time I get used to one aspect of being a parent, that particular chapter seems to close and something new opens up. There is no steady-state in all of this, and I've had to learn that being a parent means being able to land on your feet—frequently.

Virginia, the lead teacher, had her own daughter in the classroom, an arrangement that earned our instant confidence in her. Virginia is one of those people you sometimes come across who seem to be doing exactly what they set out to do in life and are loving doing it. She was technically competent, had a lot of heart, and was good at managing the other teachers and part-time college student staff as well as the infants and the parents. She was also committed that the class be the very best it could be, a goal she accomplished by rotating activities and maintaining an optimistic tone in herself and her team that was well above the required minimum. Shortly before Jack rotated out of the Chicks room, Virginia received a promotion to an administrative position. I was happy for her but thought a little magic left the classroom with her.

By now we've gotten used to Jack being in daycare, and the last and surprising benefit of his independence may be one of the biggest benefits of all: I don't feel like a failure anymore. All the way through Marisa's maternity leave, I had this nagging feeling I had somehow failed, since we couldn't afford to have her be a stay-home mom. That feeling lingered when we first put Jack in daycare. But now as I watch Jack in his new life learning to be with adults and other kids, I have come full circle. I'd had this romantic myth in my head of raising kids on a farm, listening to John Denver songs and being all together 24 hours a day. It was always in the back of my mind that Mom and Dad should be around the children all day long. Here in LA, we couldn't afford to have Marisa be a stay-at-home mom, and I thought that somehow I was short-changing Jack.

Watching Jack experience daycare has changed the way I feel about myself and about what I believe it takes to raise a human being. Up until then, I'd held onto an "us against the world" attitude, hedging each new chapter with a fair amount of fear and worry in my effort to protect our son from so many things that could harm him. Before I became a parent, I'd thought that's how my mom and dad did it, but now I am not so sure. Even though my mom stayed home with us as kids, she was never alone in raising us. Our whole town was a village that helped my parents to raise my brother, sister and me, giving us a sense of community that I only began to appreciate in retrospect.

Being a parent is changing how I look at living and also how I go about my life. It is a very humbling experience. Being a parent makes me ask for help on a daily basis, and because of that, I've discovered a new sense of connection with my human family.

Roots — April 25, 2008

I've planted several trees to commemorate Jack's birth. Back at Dad's ranch in Texas, I planted a twin Bur Oak in February of 2007, two months before Jack was born. That was the weekend when Charlie and my Texas cousins threw a surprise baby shower. When Jack was born, I planted two Sweetgum trees here in the yard of our Culver City home, one in front and one in back. The two will grow tall and have fall colors but are a special variety that is fruitless, so they won't drop the terrible sticker balls regular Sweetgums do.

This month I planted another tree, a Black Tulip Magnolia. I planted it for two reasons, the first to commemorate Jack turning one year old, and the second to honor my former college roommate Jeff's dad Ronnie, who passed away on March 8. Ronnie, who went to Texas A&M 30 years before us, who was the airline pilot who stayed extra days when he visited the campus and took the whole lot of us freshmen out to Tom's Bar BQ on Sunday evenings. He passed suddenly and he passed too soon.

Ronnie always reminded me of my dad. They both grew up in the 1950s in Texas and shared a sense of confidence, skill with tools and appreciation of the outdoors. They stayed married and loved their kids. When I learned from Humberto that Ronnie had passed, I wrote a letter to Jeff and to his mother Marge. I tried to express to them how big of an impression Ronnie had made on me back in those days, and how much I felt for them and their loss.

I went to the local nursery and found a Black Tulip Magnolia, thinking it would make a fitting tribute tree to my son and to Jeff's dad. This kind of magnolia tree is a small tree that heralds the spring with early blooming flowers. I planted it in the backyard and then after a month or two, I transplanted it to a better spot in the front yard.

I've thought about Jeff a lot, wondering how he is doing and how I would be doing in his place. Jeff loved his dad very much. Most guys have some friction with their dads, and I'm sure Jeff had his share growing up, but by the time I got to know him at A&M, there didn't seem to be much left. Jeff honored his dad, not by saying nice things about him, but by joining his father's beloved Corps of Cadets and going full out all four years. Jeff's was a living tribute to his dad. When the rest of us would be tired or lazy or cutting corners or poo-pooing some arcane Aggie tradition, it would be Jeff who would rally us with a speech about the reason for the tradition and why it mattered that we treated it with respect. It was a subtle tribute, and all the more striking because it was so low key.

Humberto lost his dad our junior year and now Jeff's dad has passed. My dad is still alive and well, and it makes me cherish him all the more. I want my friends to know I love them and I am thinking of them. I want my dad to know I love him and that I am grateful to have him to talk to and listen to. I want to be a model for my son as my dad has been to me, and as Ronnie was to Jeff and all of us.

Why has my dad been such a strong influence on me? It is his integrity. He has a way of living life that has inspired me my whole life. It's a focused way of living. It's kept him and my mother married for over 40 years. It's taken him through several careers and a four-way bypass surgery on his heart. It's let him raise three children and too many dogs to count. He delivered my sister in a station wagon and made sure both Mom and Lisa were okay. He's always been my hero.

He's very different now, and he's very much the same. That is what I love about him. He has hobbies and passions. He goes through phases of interest and exploration: model airplanes, fruit trees, gardening, ranching, farming, training dogs, exercise, wok cooking, beekeeping, shortwave radio, fishing, and backpacking. He is a hands-on guy, and loves to work with things.

I love that he loves. I mean how great is loving? Isn't it the best to be loved or to be loving, either one? I love loving, too, and how did I learn it? I got it from Dad. My loving shows itself differently probably, but how to love, how to let that lion out. *That* I got from him.

What else do I love about my dad? He's internally satisfied. While he has many interests, he has this internal satisfaction about him. It's steadying to be around him. It's calming and peaceful. He isn't out to impress anyone. He's not motivated by what others think of him.

I love how he loves his dogs. He's patient and warm with them. He'll spend hours giving haircuts or pulling out grass spurs or applying medicine. In 1997, in the dead heat of summer, sitting at a red light at the end of an Interstate off-ramp in Waco, he noticed a shivering little dog on the side of the road. The dog was on death's doorstep and very sick. Dad put on gloves, picked up the creature, placed it in a cardboard box and took it with him to the ranch. Over the next three months, he nursed the animal back to life. Hair came back, and the dog fleshed out to become a beautiful, long-haired Dachshund that he named *Booger*, because he was so bare when Dad found him. Mom renamed him *Boogie*, and he's been with us ever since. My dad has done this more than once, nurse a sick animal back into a long life, showing his compassionate nature.

I love how my dad loves my mom. They met in college on a blind date, and they've built their relationship through all these years together. They still like each other. They still love each other. They are my role models for marriage.

I love how he loves his kids. I don't think it was always the easiest thing, especially in our teenage years and through some chapters later on, but I love how he loves us, his three kids. I want to be a dad to my boy the very same way my dad was a dad to me.

There it is. That probably says more than anything else I could write. That captures everything. I want to do right by my son exactly as my dad did by me. I want to inspire my boy and be steady for him, to communicate unconditional love to my boy. Just like my dad did for me.

I heard a Catholic speaker saying recently that good parenting is loving kids most when they deserve it least, and that God's love is like that. I pray to have that kind of love as a parent. Amen to that.

As I turned the earth and prepared the soil to transplant the commemorative Black Tulip Magnolia tree, I said a little prayer and thought about my life back at Texas A&M, and about friendship and family.

Trees grow above the ground and below the ground. The leaves we see, but the roots we never see. Family is like that. My life's generations I see and know. They are the leaves that raised me with their oxygen and shade. But my ancestor's generations, I never saw nor knew. They are my roots that brought me character, the way nutrients are brought up in a tree. And though they may rest in cemeteries, their gravesites forgotten and all but lost to memory, I am still grateful for their gifts.

Having Jack and being married challenges me every day. A tree is strengthened as it bends with the wind, and I am strengthened as I learn to be patient and live life each day as a father to my son and a husband to my wife.